"My relevant identities are that I am an older white sex therapist and university instructor. I grew up in the middle of the 1965 Watts Riots surrounded by flames, fire, racism and red-lining, all of which directly impacted me and my family. Fast forward five decades, George Floyd was murdered, and I immersed myself in racial studies! I hesitate to offer my voice on this subject because I am not an expert on white supremacy, however I am an expert on what I like, and what I learn from. Carole is brilliant and this book taught me so much. I can't say enough good things about it."

Neil Cannon, *PhD, LMFT, AASECT Certified Sex Therapist &*
Supervisor, Clinical Director, The Cannon Institute

"Bold and instructive, Carole Clements has written a text that extends beyond disciplinary boundaries. It centers dysconscious racism in sexuality studies, but will benefit all white-bodied antiracist scholar-activists dedicated to interrogating white supremacy through an intersectional lens of race, sex, and gender. Storytelling supplements theoretical and practical knowledge to offer innovative and accessible strategies for inching the dial closer to justice for BIPOC through individual and collective conscientization within white institutions and communities."

Ishtar Kramer, *PhD, Core Faculty, East-West Psychology*
Department, California Institute of Integral Studies

"If ever there was a book that is deemed required reading for all White-bodied students, professors, practitioners, and those in leadership in psychotherapy, sex therapy, and sex education programs and practices, I enthusiastically and wholeheartedly recommend Clements's *Sex Positivity and White-Sex Supremacy*. Clements's work is a gallant invitation to move beyond conversation and take action."

Roger Kuhn *(Poarch Creek) PhD, LMFT, CST,*
AASECT Certified Sex Therapist

"Having co-authored two chapters with Carole on sexuality leadership and decolonizing sexuality research, I know firsthand that Carole's commitment to antiracism is unwavering, rooted in both theory and praxis. *Sex Positivity and White-Sex Supremacy: Ending Complicity in Black Body Erasure* is written in Carole's signature style: evocative, creative and candid. By incorporating mindfulness and queering, Carole offers embodied strategies for antiracist practice for white sexuality professionals. As an intuitive eating facilitator, I advocate for an embodied approach to social justice. This book makes good on that imperative. Add it to your list of must reads."

Satori Madrone, *PhD, Sexologist, Consultant, Educator*

"This book is a mirror held to the face of sex therapy as a practice in the U.S. with one crystalline question for practitioners and those who train them: Do you want to be a part of the hard work to create an anti-racist sex therapy? The practice of sex therapy has a whiteness problem as do many institutions, practices, disciplines and fields, including sexualities studies. Our continued, collective possessive investment in whiteness risks further imperiling the wellness of us all. Therapists are ethically bound to seek out and destroy the possessive investments in whiteness as it shows up in practice for the betterment of our whole society—to start, read this book."

Michelle Marzullo, *PhD, professor and Chair, Human Sexuality Department, California Institute of Integral Studies*

"Sex Positivity and White-Sex Supremacy: Ending Complicity in Black Body Erasure offers intimate and bold instruction on the issues white therapists, partners, and community members fail to see as it relates to intimate relationships. While I am not a therapist or in the sexual health field, I have learned from how Carole Clements educates the reader through the lens of White-sex Supremacy and the toxic and racist nature of sex positivity. Through research, personal story, and suggested mindfulness-based practices, the content sinks deeply into your psyche through a humble, curious, and direct voice. This book is a must-read for anyone wanting to continue their JEDI training and advance their worldview."

Licia Morelli, *founder of The Communiqué and best-selling author of* The Lemonade Hurricane *and* I Am Darn Tough

"This is mandatory reading for white sexuality counselors. Its queer antiracist lens interrogates sex positivity to offer a critical and embodied alternative that embraces *radical play*, which is how Carole teaches: meaningfully, creatively, radically."

Sorin Thomas, *MA, LPC, LAC, CGP, ACS, founding and executive director of Queer Asterisk Therapeutic Services*

"Sex Positivity and White-sex Supremacy: Ending Complicity in Black Body Erasure is a necessary contribution to how we think and talk about sex, ensuring that our commitment to sex-positive education is antiracist. On these pages, as in person, Carole Clements artfully addresses impediments to sexual inclusivity and pleasure through the lens of critical discourse, asking those of us who are white sexuality educators committed to antiracism to effort toward becoming more critically aware and embodied agents for change."

Elizabeth Wood, *MSW, CSSE, ASSECT supporting member, somatic sex educator and co-author of* The Pleasure Prescription: A Surprising Approach to Healing Sexual Pain

Sex Positivity
and White-Sex Supremacy

This text critically examines, argues, and demonstrates how the sex-positive movement is complicit in the perpetuation of White Supremacy and anti-black bias in the field of human sexualities, offering white sexuality professionals embodied ethical antiracist strategies for sexual inclusion and transformational change.

In a world where whiteness is considered the sexual and bodily norm, Carole Clements proposes that the sex-positive movement has failed to examine how it maintains White Supremacy through the guise of inclusivity, and how the lack of a critical understanding of what "sex-positive" means has caused harm to black, indigenous, and people of color (BIPOC) individuals and communities alike. Pivoting away from a sex-positive/sex-negative binary, this book establishes a sex-critical discourse by introducing and operationalizing the term "White-sex Supremacy" to produce a racially just and embodied sexual ethic. Chapters begin by looking at sexual science and its racial origins, recounting how both the science of sex and that of race strived for positivist legitimacy in the same historical moment. Moving from the social construction of racial and sexual hierarchies, chapters look at eugenics and sexology's early "sex-positive" pioneers, such as Margaret Sanger and Havelock Ellis, before examining the establishment of a race-evasive yet distinctly *white* sexual normality reliant on sex-positive framing. It shows how sex positivity became a popularized term without a clear definition other than "good," and how the legacy of white fragility leads to complicit white silence and the erasure of Black sexualities. Theoretical, practical, and accessible, it offers tangible methods for white sexuality professionals and scholars to learn accomplice ship (over allyship) to promote antiracist sexual justice activism.

This book is essential reading for white sexuality professionals, including sex educators, sex therapists, marriage and family therapists, licensed professional counselors, psychotherapists, gynecologists, and nurses, who are committed to examining their whiteness in the context of their commitment to sex positivity.

Carole Clements served as Dean of Naropa College for seven years and is Associate Professor of Contemplative Psychology at Naropa University in Boulder, Colorado, teaching graduate and undergraduate courses in Human Sexuality, Dynamics of Intimate Relationships, Erotic Intelligence and Sexual Narratives.

Leading Conversations on Black Sexualities and Identities
Series editors
James C. Wadley

Leading Conversations on Black Sexualities and Identities aims to stimulate sensitive conversations and teachings surrounding Black sexuality. Written by academics and practitioners who have dedicated their work to the distinctive sexual and relational experiences of persons of African descent, the series aims to provoke an enhanced understanding throughout the field of sexology and identify educational and clinical strategies for change. Amplifying issues and voices often minimalized and marginalized, this series is a continuation and expansion of inquiry and advocacy upon the complexities and nuances of relational negotiation, identity affirmation, critical discourse, and liberated sexual expression.

Titles in the series:

Internalized Homonegativity Among Same Gender Loving Black Men
An Exploration of Truths
by P. Ryan Grant

Sexual Health and Black College Students
Exploring the Sexual Milieu of HBCUs
Naomi M. Hall

Black Women, Intersectionality, and Workplace Bullying
Intersecting Distress
Leah P. Hollis

The Colonization of Black Sexualities
A Clinical Guide to Relearning and Healing
Anne Mauro

Sex Positivity and White-Sex Supremacy
Ending Complicity in Black Body Erasure
Carole Clements

Sex Positivity
and White-Sex Supremacy
Ending Complicity in Black
Body Erasure

Carole Clements

Routledge
Taylor & Francis Group

NEW YORK AND LONDON

First published 2024
by Routledge
605 Third Avenue, New York, NY 10158

and by Routledge
4 Park Square, Milton Park, Abingdon, Oxon, OX14 4RN

Routledge is an imprint of the Taylor & Francis Group, an informa business

Library of Congress Cataloging-in-Publication Data
Names: Clements, Carole (College teacher), author.
Title: Sex positivity and white-sex supremacy: ending complicity in Black body erasure/Carole Clements.
Description: New York, NY: Routledge, 2024. | Includes bibliographical references and index.
Identifiers: LCCN 2023011053 (print) | LCCN 2023011054 (ebook) | ISBN 9781032015750 (hardback) | ISBN 9781032039725 (paperback) | ISBN 9781003190035 (ebook)
Subjects: LCSH: Sex. | White supremacy (Social structure) | Racism against Black people.
Classification: LCC HQ21. C587 2024 (print) | LCC HQ21 (ebook) | DDC 306.7—dc23/eng/20230321
LC record available at https://lccn.loc.gov/2023011053
LC ebook record available at https://lccn.loc.gov/2023011054

ISBN: 978-1-032-01575-0 (hbk)
ISBN: 978-1-032-03972-5 (pbk)
ISBN: 978-1-003-19003-5 (ebk)

DOI: 10.4324/9781003190035

Typeset in Times New Roman
by Apex CoVantage, LLC

To Gianna

Contents

1   White Supremacy and Sex: Historicity and Home

2   Ghosts in the Kitchen: The Present Absent of Whiteness

Acknowledgments

Writing a book is often a lonely but never solitary process. Buoying me here, as in life, is a colorful and cherished cast of characters. I mention only some of you here, with heartfelt gratitude:

To James Wadley, for your vision and generosity; especially, for taking a chance on me.

To my editors at Routledge, Heather Evans and Jana Craddock, for your kindness and patience.

To my students at Naropa University, to whom I first presented the critical concept of White-sex Supremacy. Your engaging presence is the joy in my teaching.

To Licia Morelli, for your kind-keen eye, and for reading every word. What a treat it is to circle back with you and revisit senior seminaresque magic!

To Michelle Marzullo, who first introduced me (like a virgin) to queer temporality and my queer theorist crushes (e.g., Butler, Halberstam, Muñoz); and for validating my queer way of knowing in a straight field. You reflect that I am more humanities than social sciences, more poetry than empirical research. Because of you, I can trust my mind.

To Sorin Thomas, who like me cannot think straight.

To Susan Burggraf, for being my Go-To "Jesus."

To Ineta and Pedro, for loving me when I could not love myself.

To my mom, for being here even when I cannot.

And to my partner, Terry Allison, who gave me my heart's desire—room to fly!

Foreword

When I discussed Carole's research and advocacy efforts around ending complicity in Black-body erasure, I was unsure about how it would resonate with those who might subscribe or have interest in the *Leading Conversations About Black Sexualities and Identities* series. I think it was difficult for me to get out of my own way of learning and expanding my concept of race and allowing someone who does not identify as Black or African descent to be a part of this initiative. One of Carole's identities is white, and my initial thought was to be exclusionary (based on race) and not offer an opportunity for me (us) to learn. As a Black man who has grown up in the shadows of White Supremacy, there are days when it feels like I've learned, lived, and had enough. Somewhere though, I realized that I needed to be more open to differences because learning from one another can truly be seen as a gift.

When Carole submitted the first manuscript, I was blown away at the level of insight, experience, and self-awareness Carole has navigating family, professional, and social circumstances that center whiteness as the norm. Carole's sense of humility is remarkable. Using personal experiences, Carole invites us to think expansively about black-body erasure and its influence on Black sexualities and identities.

Carole's book is art. Carole gives our community an opportunity to examine and re-examine black-body erasure in how whiteness is managed or mismanaged and the privileges that are associated with being white. One could argue that this book may not have a place within this series, but similar to most paintings in art museums or songs included on music albums, Carole's work is special and has its own merit as a medium for interpretation and growth. I hope that as you read this book, you are able to learn and grow as so many others have when they encounter Carole's work.

James C. Wadley, Ph.D.

Preface

2 Future: Dead End

The one thing I wanted as a child, but never got, was *to fly*.

"Now is not the time to imagine that I am a bird about to take flight, or a winged angel ascending to the heaven. My task is to remain fully present to the experience of the here and now" (Bellerose, 2018, p. 58).

The idea for this book crystalized within a particular *spacetime*—following the livestreamed (initially thought-to-be) eight-minute 46-second murder of George Floyd (which we will learn takes agonizingly longer) on May 25, 2020, during an apex of the coronavirus pandemic when most white Americans were shuttered in, watching the horror unfold from the safety of their homes as non-essential workers. Their lives were further disrupted by the contagion of racial virulence that seemed to have newly entered their consciousness as a lethal pathogen. Their outrage sparked a fervent, albeit fleeting, white wake-up call: my phone rang and pinged with queries from white friends and colleagues—many of whom are sex educators and therapists—for recommendations on how best to learn about and check their white privilege so as to stop anti-Black violence from recurring, despite its historically and systemically entrenched roots. The idea that racism and anti-Blackness exist beyond personal prejudice, within law enforcement and judicial and carceral systems designed to "protect," was eye-opening for many of my white friends and colleagues. For a moment in spacetime, Black outrage became viscerally acknowledged in some white bodies. Bodily discomfort around racial injustice routinely present became amplified in my own body as well as I listened to my Black stepdaughter justifiably rage against the historical inaction and silent complicity of too many whites.

My experience as a white person tells me that white people being willing or wanting to talk about *white privilege*, *White Supremacy*, *white fragility*, *white rage* (topics I am familiar with as a critical sexuality scholar) is atypical. More typical are reactions of ignorance, denial, defensiveness, outrage, and blame when the topic of whiteness—White Supremacy in particular—is broached. If, as a white reader, you require that I convince you Write Supremacy exists in all quarters of American life, then this book is likely not for you. If, however, you are aware of its existence—its tenacious grip and stronghold—and would like to learn what to do about it ethically as a white sexuality professional, then settle in. This book *is* for you. It is designed to help facilitate conversations about anti-Blackness in our field and our complicity with it.

This requires that as *Whitepeople* we talk among ourselves—in reflective conversation—*before* engaging with our colleagues of color. First, we must acknowledge that we cannot stand apart from our race, which I underscore by referencing "Whitepeople" to affix whiteness to us when we may want to disavow it. *White* is not an adjective or a modifier in this case; it is an identifiable class of privileged *White*people who are systemically complicit in White Supremacy and thus responsible for (and capable of) its undoing.

Whitepeople

Although white people—like all people—are *heterogenous* and *singular* in their individual expressions, I employ the term *Whitepeople* throughout the book to emphasize the performativity and homogeneity of whiteness, and to underscore that Whitepeople are the topmost caste (Wilkerson, 2020). *Whitepeople perform whiteness* based on the overarching authority of White Supremacy—a term I also capitalize (along with Whiteculture and Whiteworld) to accentuate the omniscient *God*-like reach and power of whiteness, with the authority to determine who lives or dies.

Whiteness is born of White Supremacy, given that racism precedes race (Coates, 2015; Painter, 2010). It is the antithesis of Blackness, which I also capitalize throughout, to respect that "black" is not a color of people but the cultural experience of *being Black* within an inescapable caste system of White Supremacy in the United States. For this reason, when I refer to whiteness, I do not capitalize it, because I want to lower its status.

Broaching Whiteness

To be responsible for our whiteness—and our complicity with White Supremacy—we must *broach* it. In counseling, broaching is defined as the "effort to discuss the racial, ethnic, and cultural (REC) issues that are relevant to the client's presenting concerns" (Day-Vines et al., 2021, p. 348). Broaching involves deliberately acknowledging diversity (e.g., race, ethnicity, nationality, gender, sexuality, ability, age, and socioeconomic status) as a means for offering culturally responsive care and establishing safety and rapport with clients (Day-Vines et al., 2007, 2020, 2021). Broaching is meant to invite open communication, including self-disclosure, to reassure those in therapy that diversity in its myriad forms is welcome, establishing the basis for trust and the capacity (of the educator, counselor, therapist, etc.) to competently address the sociocultural context and lived experiences of privilege and oppression. Research demonstrates that omission of broaching results in microaggressions. When white sexuality professionals fail to broach their whiteness (and its privilege), harm may occur (Madrone & Clements, 2021).

Broaching whiteness and White Supremacy following George Floyd's murder became a common occurrence on my Facebook feed by many of my white friends. Suddenly, White Supremacy became relevant to *Whitepeople's* psychological wellness. Tragically, it took the livestreamed murder of an un-armed Black man—pleading *I can't breathe* to the white cop with a knee on his neck—to recognize the physical and psychological cost of White Supremacy *for Whitepeople*, not just Black people.

This book *broaches* the sexual consequences of White Supremacy, given how race, gender, and sex have been weaponized under colonization, with *traces* of White-supremacist sexual violence and fragility evident today, including within sex-positive discourses. It examines how the racist sexual violence that is White Supremacy (Brown, 2008; Stokes, 2001), introduced here as *White-sex Supremacy*, manifests discursively and performatively in white bodies in **sp**ace, ***place***, and ***time***, referred to as "splacetime."

Splacetime

Splacetime (as I conceive it) = Spacetime + Place, including three dimensions of space (height, width, depth), plus place, plus time. Physicists conceive of *universal spacetime* by releasing their subjective experience of it to gain broader perspective, which is what I am asking you to do. If you are white, suspend your subjective experience. Invite curiosity and pause. Notice what arises in the somatic and geographic *between space*. Refrain from solidifying knowingness. I ask this because as inheritors of White-sex Supremacy we erase Black bodies through White-supremacist, race-evasive, (dis)embodied, sex-positive discourses that perform white (sexual) nervousness (Beard, 1880, 1881, 1884), referred to as *white fragility* today (DiAngelo, 2011, 2018). The discomfort of not knowing causes us to claim certainty, and we become urgent, graspy, and harmful. To address this, I offer *Radical Play Acts* for white readers to disrupt their complicity with White-sex Supremacy and practice broaching their white racial privilege in new and uncomfortable ways.

Multiculturalism's Failure

Typically, broaching does not directly interrogate White Supremacy or its *present absence* in the field of human *sexualities* (deliberately referred to as plural rather than singular given the complex multiplicities of sex) and what I aim to rectify here. Multicultural policies and practices designed to support justice, equity, diversity, and inclusion (JEDI) fall short without direct interrogation of omnipresent systems of oppression designed to appear absent (Brown, 2008; Iantaffi, 2012; Dottolo & Kaschak, 2015). This failure is largely due to the fact that whiteness does not see itself as staring back in the mirror (Hare-Mustin, 1994). Whiteness misinterprets its reflection as *universal* rather than *relative*—as *all* people, rather than *White*people. Hence, the rebuttal *All Lives Matter* at the suggestion Black Lives *also* do.

Black Lives Matter

Multiculturalism often involves Whitepeople teaching Whitepeople how to relate to Black Indigenous People of Color (BIPOC), rather than centering the voices and experiences of those who have been marginalized by White Supremacy. The multicultural initiatives in the post-Civil Rights Era expanded beyond racial justice to include justice for other marginalized constituencies (e.g., ciswomen, same-sex loving, transgender individuals, and people with disabilities) such that the focus became more diffuse. As race became less prominent in the multicultural movement, justice for Black people was impeded. Hence, the necessary reminder: *Black Lives Matter*.

In the aftermath of George Floyd's public lynching, there seemed to be momentary agreement among Blacks *and* whites that anti-Black racism must be addressed, evident in the historic turnout of Whitepeople protesting *against* police violence and *for* Black Lives, including in mostly white rural towns like Sandpoint, Idaho, Norwood, Colorado, Harlan, Kentucky, and Ontario, Oregon, where few (if any) Black people live (Muller, 2020). This tenuous alliance in the splacetime continuum where polarized political factions during a divisive Trump presidency appeared less oppositional and more humane, if only briefly, was for me a welcome tear in the sturdy fabric of American *civilization*—a White-supremacist discourse aimed at "civilizing savages" (meaning those who are not white) by erecting a hierarchical system of Bad-Better-Best masquerading as "democracy" that Isabel Wilkerson (2020) refers to as *caste*, which is first and foremost racialized, then gendered and sexed.

That this "civilized" human taxonomy—inspiring red MAGA hats, alternative facts, Fake News, conspiracy theories, anti-science, racist law-and-order rhetoric, and a US Capitol insurrection—is maintained and reinforced through White-supremacist lay and professional sexual discourses, including civilization discourse, normality discourse, erotic love and marriage discourse, and sex positivity discourse (the focus here), may be revelatory to many white sexuality educators and therapists who consider themselves *woke*. Specifically, this book is for them. While this is likely not news for Black sexuality professionals, (re)perceiving White Supremacy as functioning discursively and performatively as *present absence* in space, place, and time (i.e., splacetime) may be useful, though I will respectfully let them be the deciders of that.

Sex Positivity

Despite its optimism, sex positivity can be negating. Worse, it can be racist—complicit in White-sex Supremacy. Sex positivity is often cursorily adopted by "well-meaning" white sexuality professionals, who assume that *sexual liberation* is a matter of personal consent rather than the systemic outcome of power inequities. That sexuality should be inclusive is a key feature of sex positivity but also misleading, given that White Supremacy is rarely discussed in sex-positive discourses. In fact, not one book or journal article centering sex positivity that I read in preparation for this project interrogated (or even mentioned) White Supremacy, though all advocated for diversity and inclusion.

Sex positivity requires critical scrutiny and a comprehensive definition, which is currently lacking in the literature (Ivanski & Kohut, 2017). I do not offer a comprehensive definition of sex positivity here. Rather, I introduce the critical concept of White-sex Supremacy to interrogate discursive sex positivity for its racist past and present.

Literature on sex positivity implies that consent between adults is a "high" bar when it is a precariously low one (Glickman, 2019). We might consult radical feminists from the 1970s, who lost the porn wars arguing how personal consent does not take systems of oppression (e.g., patriarchy) and their effects on different bodies into account when considering "who" possesses the *privilege to consent.*

The presumption that sex positivity's positiveness applies to *all* people is misguided. For example, historically, heterosexual sex among Whitepeople (Anglo-Saxon protestants to be exact) was intended to literally *reproduce* Whiteculture. Arguably, this is still the case. Unless we critically examine how *not* to reproduce Whiteculture through discursive White-sex, sex positivity will continue to propagate whiteness, erasing Black bodies and sexualities in the process.

What Is White?

As the proverbial water fish swim in, whiteness easily goes unnoticed, unchecked, and/or ignored by those it benefits most, meaning Whitepeople. Whiteness refers to those with light skin and those who benefit from light-skin privilege. Ironically, the hyper-visibility of whiteness leads to its invisibility. Whitepeople typically refer to "non-whites" as *groups* (e.g., Blacks, people of color) but to ourselves as *individuals*, implying that we lack racial identity or that it is inconsequential. Notably, the term "person of color" was adopted by racial justice advocates in the late twentieth century to resist *minoritization*, including terms like "non-white" that discursively affirm the superiority of Whitepeople (Sen, 2007).

Whiteness is glib. Cheerful in its denial: *Oh no, I'd never. That's not me. I couldn't possibly. You see, I care. I have Black friends and family. My spouse, friend, lover, child is Black.* Going further: *What can I do? Tell me, I want to help. Can I touch your hair? You don't act/look/sound Black. You're actually pretty.* Whiteness has consequences. It threatens physical *dis*-ease that white bodies—my own included—seek to shirk. The physiological impact of whiteness is accentuated in the term White-*body* Supremacy (Menakem, 2017), a concept I utilize here to underscore how White-sex Supremacy is *embodied*—occupying *minds* (as beliefs and ideologies) and *bodies* (as neurobiological responses to trauma) to establish a kind of *theatrical whiteness* in which the *present absence of White Supremacy* (detailed later) is performed through (dis)embodied white discomfort and white fragility (DiAngelo, 2011, 2018) centering sex.

White Supremacy is also dimensional, filling space, place, and time (i.e., splacetime) as *objects* (e.g., nooses, burning crosses, history books), *locations* (e.g., gentrified neighborhoods, evangelical churches, the dark web), and *motion* (e.g., chattel slavery, rape, white knees on Black necks). Black bodies have no choice but to navigate the danger and trespass of White Splacetime. Their lives depend on it. With White-supremacist violent extremism on the rise, Black bodies are especially vulnerable (Racially and Ethnically Motivated Violent Extremism, 2021).

Opening 19 years ago in a Black community and food desert, Tops Supermarket on Buffalo's east side (just west of where I grew up) compelled a White-supremacist gunman to target it on May 14, 2022. "An avowed racist, he selected this Tops after researching predominantly Black ZIP codes and drove hundreds of miles here from his nearly all-white hometown" (Wilson, 2022, para. 9) to murder Black people.

The connection between bodies, race, space, place, and time is an intimate one (Borren, 2019) requiring reflexive examination by Whitepeople, whose modus operandi regarding race is typically one of *dis*-embodiment—where embodiment and racial awareness diverge, causing dissociated panic (i.e., nervousness), defensiveness and denial, such that White-body supremacy manifests as White Fragility (DiAngelo, 2011, 2018).

Turning White

In her blogpost titled "The Spatial Phenomenology of White Embodiment" Marieke Borren (2019), a Dutch expatriate, encounters the *facticity of white embodiment* in 2015, when she temporarily moves to the predominantly Black city of Johannesburg, South Africa.

> Previously, living in my native country, I was colorless, blending in with my environment to the point of being unnoticeable. In my new city of residence, I suddenly became a member of a minority group—white

people—which meant I stood out, visibly, in public space. Seeing non-white others see me as white, first made me see myself as white, too.

(para. 1)

Like Borren, I "turned white" in the 1980s, in the aftermath of being sexually assaulted in my college dorm room by a white cisgender male student. This singular event tilted my world on its axis, turning it (and me) upside down. I was catapulted out of the familiarity and (perceived) safety of my "idyllic" Whiteworld to "slum it" (as my father would say) with first-generation Black and Brown college friends from the South Bronx, Harlem, Jamaica, Queens, Wilmington, Delaware, and Alexandria, Virginia—all of whom knew, before I could grok it myself, the intensity of rage I felt toward the *Whiteman.* Like other socialized Whitewomen, I had been duped into believing that I was fragile, and that it was the Whiteman's duty to protect me, (mis)shaping my sexuality. I was named Carole but raised as "Karen" (a pejorative term to describe a demanding and entitled white women) replete with a White-supremacist sexual narrative and consciousness that highlighted my racialized "sexual superiority" via white beauty standards (e.g., blue-green eyes and strawberry-blonde hair) and white feminine sexual "purity" and "fragility." Rather than question this White-supremacist sexual narrative, I believed it to be *true.* My first conscious memory of it was when I was nine years old and asked my parents if I could visit my new crush, who played piano and lived on Steuben Street in Utica, New York. Their answer was a quick and unequivocal "No" (a rarity for them) because Steuben, they explained, was on the Other (a.k.a., Bad-Black) Side of Town.

As traumatic as my rape had been—witnessed by Khadijah Jahn, my Saudi Arabian roommate, whose disgust seared into me from atop her bunk across the room as my date penetrated me despite my repeated (albeit drunken) pleas not to, causing me to dissociate from my body and float upward toward the ceiling—nothing prepared me for the betrayal I felt by Whiteculture, consisting of my white family and friends who could neither understand nor handle my rage. In the face of it, they grew defensive. Initially, I did what I was trained to do as a *Whitewoman:* I collapsed. Until, that is, I was buoyed by newfound friendships with people of color.

Gender serves as a vehicle for maintaining White Supremacy by defining the parameters of (white cisgender) maleness and (white cisgender) femaleness, and (white) femininity and (white) masculinity—establishing what it means to be a "real" man or woman, from which toxic (white) masculinity and fragile (white) femininity are constructed. I did not have a term for the disembodiment I felt as a white socialized female in the aftermath of being raped by a Whiteman—discursively designed to be the protector of my (white) sexual purity—until I was embraced by my Black and Brown friends, who knew firsthand the trauma and rage of White Supremacy, and therefore did not recoil from mine. My Black and Brown friends offered me comfort that my white friends did not. For example, when I was losing grip on my sanity, Paul held me while I sobbed through the night. Upon awakening he encouraged me to get help, kindly but adamantly insisting that I was *not* okay. Ineta held my hands and gaze in compassion not judgment when I revealed the sordid details of my sexual assault. Pedro understood that my inclination to seek refuge in sex with strangers was hurting more than helping me. I can hear his voice echoing through the decades, as if he was talking to me now from inside the tub in the bathroom at his parent's home on East Tremont Street in the South Bronx, while I am sitting on the tile floor facing in the opposite direction to give him privacy as he bathed, "Clements, you got to keep your legs shut." His voice was stern and loving, not slut-shaming.

From my Black and Brown friends, I learned that my sexual trauma was interwoven with the trauma of White Supremacy, which would take years of therapy to further unpack. In hindsight, it is likely what unconsciously led me to become a therapist myself.

Hiding in Plain Sight

My personal and professional therapeutic journey has revealed that racial recognition is a slow process under white privilege, because White Supremacy *hides in plain sight*—behind slogans of *All Lives Matter* and race-evasive sex-positive discourses. Whiteness also employs ethnicity as a form of racial bypass.

Ethnic Underground

Walking into the basement of a Catholic Church years ago while visiting my godmother in Alexandria Bay, New York, looking for the bathroom, I stumbled upon a group of Polish-American church ladies preparing muffins and coffee for an after-mass social. "Can I help you?" one of them asked, eyeing me suspiciously. Once identifying who I "belonged" to—that is, my godmother, a well-known member of the church community, who was praying upstairs (presumably establishing my "right" to be there)—the church lady hopped up to warmly greet me, excitedly sharing that she too is Polish, nearly accosting me with her ethnic exuberance: *It's the best thing to be! I wouldn't want to be anything else. I feel sorry for people who aren't like us.*

Gobsmacked by her Polish pride, I recomposed myself to refocus my attention on finding the bathroom. The aroma of freshly brewing coffee (a smell I have always detested) wafted through the room. Suddenly, I felt nauseated by all that was brewing, including how swooped up, taken in, accepted I was, for no other reason than being *Polish*, which in this case is synonymous with being *white*. When she finally pointed in the direction of the bathroom, I politely thanked her (concealing my upset; a very "white" thing to do, making me complicit) while hoping that my Black partner and stepson—who were upstairs praying alongside my godmother—would not need to use the bathroom, given they are neither Polish nor white, and therefore did not—*could not*—belong.

My basement encounter with the prideful Polish church lady is palpable recognition that White Supremacy permeates predominantly white spaces like the smell of freshly brewing coffee, which gagged me until I grew accustomed to it brewing in our home. White Supremacy disguised as ethnicity is impactful due to its subtly, which in actuality is as well-worn as the blue-gray industrial carpet I walked across to pee, and as disruptive as the weeping willow tree in my Ciocia ("aunt" in Polish) Stella's backyard, with its invasive yet invisible root system threatening to destroy the plumbing, clogging pipes with human excrement.

Racial Bypass

What I observed in that church basement years ago, I have witnessed countless times before and since: the strategic bypassing of racial responsibility amid predominantly white yet ethnically diverse communities, like the one I grew up in.

Little to no recognition of white privilege—let alone *supremeness*—was a prominent feature of my childhood community, comprised of previously *non-whites*, mainly Italians, Poles (my ethnicity), Irish, Lebanese, and Bosnians, who have been culturally allowed to assimilate. In the high school I attended with approximately 1,500 students, *maybe* three were Black. Whiteness was rarely, if ever, discussed.

Despite mighty insistence *There's no racism here!* it cracked through, like the tenacious roots of Ciocia Stella's weeping willow, upending the pristine sidewalks of our slice of Americana. As teenagers we partied in the woods on Gibson Road, nicknamed the *N-word Road*, which we used unabashedly. Even now, decades later, I cannot easily get my friends to talk about it. We were racially privileged white kids who never questioned why we called it that, or even if we *should*. Afterall, ours was a community that prided itself on being hardworking middle class, which translated to Good People, not *uppity* or *white*. And yet routinely I heard people say: *Don't act N-word rich. Stay away from the Bad (a.k.a. "Black") part of town.* No one considered that our thoughts, behaviors, and comments were racist and responsible for inscribing White Supremacy into the future that our children's children will inherit.

Dead Futures

Like a House of Cards, White Supremacy creates a *splatial* architecture: a literal and figurative space-place (like the woods we partied in) that despite its rickety base has endured for centuries. I was raised in that House of Cards, in the *only* structure on a street named *Future*—which ironically (and also fittingly) is a Dead End—in a suburb named *Whites*boro, adjacent to *Whites*town, on land stolen from the On^yoteaka and the Haudenosaunee, in a county named Oneida in the Mohawk Valley in Central New York. Perhaps this, more than anything, has shaped me—inspiring me to write this book all these years later.

One day the town's municipality put up a Stop! sign at the end of our street, as if to emphasize the point: the Future of White Boroughs is Dead.

Despite my incessant childhood yearning to flap imaginal wings and take flight from the roof of my parents' house on Future, my high-arched feet (the only body parts that resemble a "classic" dancer) remain planted, as if flat-footed (like my partner's feet—another of our striking distinctions) firmly on the ground, for better or worse, in *this* Here-Now House of Cards.

This book is one small attempt to rouse the wind in splacetime and blow that house apart.

Introduction

Privilege, Power, and Play

The overarching goal of this book is meant to serve as an introduction to the relevancy of Black sexuality for white sexuality professionals, who might otherwise not read the books in this series, which I believe is critical reading for practicing ethically, especially when the population white sexuality practitioners serve is also predominantly white. Otherwise, white sexuality professionals are poised to perpetuate White Supremacy through sex-positive discourses that advocate for inclusivity but remain dysconsciously race-evasive. Ethical practice compels us beyond regulatory rule-following to *doing what is right* (Watter, 2012), namely interrogating White Supremacy.

"'The time has come,' the Walrus said, 'To talk of many things: Of shoes—and ships—and sealing-wax—Of cabbages—and kings—And why the sea is boiling hot—and whether pigs have wings'" (Carroll, 1871/2019, p. 29). Indeed, the time has come for Whitepeople to talk about White Supremacy. *Really* talk—as if pigs have wings: to (re)imagine the world upside down instead of right side up, such that the topsy-turviness of the COVID-19 global pandemic, (re)exposing racial fissures (e.g., economic and health-care disparities) can be repurposed to effectuate transformational change, including within the field of human sexualities, because the sea has been boiling for centuries with ghosts of Black bodies (dead and alive) thrown overboard, during the transatlantic steal to a godforsaken New World. Like seafoam, the fomenting toxicity of whiteness reached shore, sprouting sea legs on land to balance unsteadily at first, then steadier and steadier still, until supplanted solidly—*imperially*—in this soil in every nook and cranny as Supreme Heir (i.e., The King).

Because of this, an upside-down imperative using queer (anti)logic (Eng, 2010; Halberstam, 2011) to disrupt and dismantle normative assumptions is needed for dislodging White Supremacy—especially when it comes to sex and its (mis)shapen whiteness. That is my attempt here: to articulate how White-sex Supremacy functions in splacetime then (re)perceive it queerly toward ending complicity in the erasure of Black bodies. To do this, we must recognize how discursive sex positivity serves as a smokescreen for white sexuality professionals to hide behind. We must interrogate *our relationship*

DOI: 10.4324/9781003190035-1

with our racial privilege—the *conferred power* of whiteness—and learn how to "play" with it more skillfully (i.e., radically) to ameliorate harm, until the White-supremacist sexual caste system that maintains sexual racism is thoroughly dismantled.

What Is (White)

It is not enough to acknowledge What Is without changing What Is when it is harmful.

During this unprecedented time of disruption and uncertainty, examining and responding to *What Is* are fundamental for societal change and transformation, particularly with regard to racism and its stalwart anti-Blackness, requiring the educational and clinical strategies to get there in the field of human sexualities, hence the need for a book series on *Leading Conversations about Black Sexualities and Identities.* This book is only one in the series, meant to be useful for white sexuality professionals aspiring toward *accomplice*-ship (Osler, n.d.) and antiracist *action* not just feel-good ideological lip service.

Following George Floyd's public execution—amid international outcry against white-on-Black violence—many white sexuality professionals began asking in earnest how to uncover and disrupt their racist complicity toward the facilitation of needed and lasting systemic change. This book serves as one response to their request. It is intended to rouse and guide white sexuality educators, therapists, counselors, coaches, scholars, and so on, toward interrogating and dismantling (rather than performing and sustaining) white racial dominance that is steeped in sexual violence, a primary source of anti-Blackness. This requires the willingness to examine White-supremacist sexual discourses and performativity and engage in Radical Play Acts to uncover how White-sex Supremacy is maintained through the cursory adoption of sex-positive rhetoric under the guise of inclusivity, with little to no examination of what it means to be *white* and *fragile* in this field.

This book introduces White-sex Supremacy as a critical concept for interrogating sex positivity to reveal the historical underpinnings of *white fragility* (DiAngelo, 2011, 2018) and demonstrate how an *unexamined ethic* of sex positivity becomes complicit in the erasure of Black sexualities. It utilizes *splacetime* as a conceptual mechanism to (re)perceive how White-sex Supremacy manifests in racialized space, place, and time to facilitate racial awareness and justice in a field beleaguered by White-supremacist sexual discourse and *performative fragility.*

To this end, Chapter 1 examines the impact that White Supremacy and white fragility have on sex and sexuality in the United States to re-*right* history through the application of *historicity* based on historical actuality rather than White-supremacist myth. *Regimes of historicity* (Hartog, 2015) serve as the vantage point from which to (re)perceive and develop reconciliatory awareness toward accepting responsibility for the sexual violence of discursive and performative *white* sex, referred to here as *White-sex Supremacy*.

Chapter 2 illuminates the *absent presence* of ghosts, meaning those who were colonized and sexually violated through chattel slavery. The discursive weaponry of the colonizers ensures that the *present absence of whiteness* is endemic to discursive sex, including sex positivity. Overt and covert traces of White Supremacy permeate American culture, with artifacts of colonization and whiteness inhabiting our homes. White readers will be asked to take an inventory of the White-supremacist artifacts in their homes while engaging this book.

Chapter 3 reveals failure: Whitepeople's failure, queer failure, my failure, and what I erased while writing this book and its inconsequential loss when juxtaposed with the erasure of Black bodies.

Chapter 4 demonstrates how time is socially constructed, meaning gendered, sexed, and raced. We will learn it is common for different individuals, groups, and communities to live during the same historical periods, yet have vastly different experiences of those times, referred to as *synchronous nonsynchronicity* (Bloch, 1935/1991), which is applicable to white heteronormative time that forms the basis of discursive White sex.

Chapter 5 shows the historical link between the science of race and the science of sex, introducing the concept of *splacetime* in more detail, where anti-Black racism is (re)enacted and White-sex Supremacy is performed through habituated and racist sexual scripts.

Chapter 6 highlights the raced, sexed, and gendered bodily hierarchy that is *corporeal theatrics* to construct *White-sex Theater*, where white sexual scripting and performativities shape (dis)embodied racist sexual tension in splacetime.

Chapter 7 encourages presence and radical play, introducing the Five Eye Practices (Dilley, 2015) and other embodied activities to elicit heterodoxy for countering White-sex Supremacy.

Still, the question remains: "Why do we need another representation of whiteness in conversation with itself?"

Why Whiteness? Why Here?

In *The Heart of Whiteness: Normal Sexuality and Race in America, 1880–1840*, Julian Carter (2007) addresses this question by stating, "an exploration of white-absorption is not the same thing as a performance of it" (p. 44). The distinction is critical. White Supremacy is performed routinely and subtly in our field, yet too many "well-meaning" white sexuality professionals remain unaware of their culpability. This book aims to change that amid valid argument that a book focused on whiteness should *not* be included in a series dedicated to Black sexualities and identities, which is exactly the critical feedback I received early on.

Tabbing Conversations

Books are conversations, though admittedly the timeframe over which they are written can be problematic, as it takes time for books to come to fruition. Books are also arguably one-sided—more monologue than dialogue—at least initially, aside from early peer-reviewed feedback and editorial critique. Eventually, however, books become public spaces in which conversations ensue, sparking curiosity, speculation, inspiration, disagreement, argument, criticism, and so on.

A former student of mine, having seen me carry armfuls to class, asked that I bequeath him my books when I die—each color-coded with multicolored sticky tabs that index my thinking on the subject, which I write on with permanent marker to highlight what strikes me: what to wrestle with, think further about, make comparisons with, and draw parallels to. This book is an invitation for you to do likewise: *Tab*—figuratively and/or literally—as you chew, mull, criticize, eye roll, and rebut. In doing so, you keep tabs on me. First, however, I want to clarify that I am not looking for you to "like" this book; it is not a social media post, no emojis necessary. This means I will not be offended if you do not like it, or if you criticize what I have to say, or disagree. I repeatedly tell students that I never assign readings for them to *like*, but to grapple with, to push their knowledge to the edges of their meaning-making, so their learning becomes *developmental* rather than regurgitative—integrating meaning *and* sense.

Critical Reflexivity

Contemplative education at Naropa University, where I am a professor, is embodied. Naropa's namesake, an abbot of Nalanda University in Northern India in the eleventh century, with the help of his teacher Tilopa, distinguishes between *meaning* and *sense*, also referred to as *knowledge* and *wisdom*. Sense integrates meaning to extend beyond the mere memorization of facts toward the development of embodied wisdom.

Sense-making requires *critical reflection*, including the purposeful examination of values, ethics, feelings, behaviors, and motives—in this case, vis-à-vis my proximity to racialized power. *Critical reflexivity*—interrelated and distinguishable from critical reflection—is also necessary, given its focus on the *discursive construction* of reality, including societal norms, systems, and power relations (Ng et al., 2019).

Superficially Sex-Positive

The ethical adoption of a sex-positive mindset by well-meaning white sexuality professionals is meant to circumvent the harmful effects of sex negativity. Rarely, however, do white sexuality professionals examine the discursive

White-supremacist construction of sex positivity, making its adoption cursory, resulting in dysconscious racism. "Because sexuality and sex therapy are so heavily influenced by the values and morals of its practitioners, we must continuously examine and debate the ethical issues related to the directions and interventions the field chooses to take" (Watter, 2012, p. 87) to generate transformational personal and systemic change. Our individual and collective ill-preparedness as Whitepeople—including our uncritical and non-reflexive habits of mind—is evident in the prevalence of white heterosexism in our field and the superficial adoption of sex positivity.

Do No Harm

Ethically, *doing no harm* is insufficient because it operates passively. Whereas *doing what is right* is active, even when what is "right" is unclear (i.e., a guess or approximation) (Watter, 2012). As white sexuality professionals, we must develop critical reflexivity by examining how we talk about sex, including *positive* sex. As a white sexuality professional, I was challenged to be critically reflective and reflexive when proposing a book for this series.

Reviewer C

This book was in early conversation during its proposal phase with three anonymous peer reviewers, whose attention and generosity I am grateful for. Each provided a nugget for me to chew on: shaping the direction of this book and deepening my meaning-and-sense making. Reviewer C, an academic and clinician of color (as they self-identified), was particularly critical and thus helpful to me, disagreeing that this book should be included in the series. Identifying as "not white," they expressly stated that they are "not interested in another book on white reactions to the empowerment of Black people." Understandably. Enough *is* enough.

I do not know who Reviewer C is, but if they ever wish to introduce themselves, I would welcome it, as their critical feedback pushed me in the direction I have gone here. Even when falling short (presuming I have) this will not be a *dysconscious* recentering of whiteness. Rather, my focus is the eradication of Black-body erasure and sexual racism in our field using critical reflexivity.

Dysconscious Racism

Uncritical habits of mind form the basis of *dysconscious racism*, described as the unexamined adoption of hegemonic norms and privileges—amid microaggressions—embedded in systems and practices that perpetuate White Supremacy and race-based inequities (Anderson et al., 2019; Sue et al.,

2009; King, 1991) central to our work here. As a critical concept, White-sex Supremacy highlights the *present absence of whiteness* and its role in the erasure of Black bodies and sexualities through racist and race-evasive sex-positive discourses.

As a conscientizing mechanism, I offer Radical Play Acts throughout for confronting white privilege, upending assumptions, and helping us (re)perceive. Take the time to engage them:

- Notice your discomfort.
- Welcome your awkwardness.
- Develop habits of mind that move you from dysconsciousness to critically reflective and reflexive awareness.

Always-Already in the Room

Returning to the question: *Why is a book focusing on whiteness included in a series dedicated to leading conversations in Black sexualities and identities?* Perhaps the simplest answer is because White Supremacy is *always-already* in the room. When co-presenting *The Shadow Side of Sex Positivity: Uncovering the White Fragility Taboo* at the American Association for Sex Educators, Counselors, and Therapists (AASECT) in June 2018, I acknowledged that whiteness is "embedded in the carpet like cat pee." It stinks and is hard to remove.

Blondie

I am speaking with a prospective client, a formerly incarcerated cisgender heterosexual Black man, about the idea of sex therapy. "I'm not supposed to be here, talking with you," he says. "I grew up in the hood. Schooled on the street about women and sex. I was told to get me a Blondie." (For the sake of "status" and/or "credibility" I presume, though I choose not to ask because I do not want to interrupt him.) He goes on to explain that in prison you get two choices: "You have sex with guys—be 'homosexual'—or you hide," explaining:

> You get in trouble if you get caught, so you got to be sneaky. Yeah, let's talk infidelity. I've always been left. By my pops. My baby mama, she just up and left. Don't get me wrong, I want to learn, grow. But yeah man, White supremacy fucked me up. Taught me how I'm not supposed to be here.

His stream of consciousness, which I truncate here, was prompted by my acknowledgment that I am white. Not a Blondie, but close. I am a redhead with alabaster skin. When working with clients and students who are BIPOC, I believe it is my ethical responsibility to say two things up front: first, stating the obvious (which rarely gets said): *I am white.* Second, *White Supremacy is* (always-already) *in the room with us, especially when we talk about relationships and sex.*

Radical Play Act

• **Reflect on and practice saying aloud:**

  • *I am white.*
  • *White Supremacy is always in the room when we talk about intimacy, sex, and relationships.*

Why say these two things? Because stating What Is matters, especially when *What Is White* is not typically acknowledged, especially by Whitepeople in the room. "White is the color of the colonizer; black, brown, yellow, and red, the colors of the colonized. This is the embodiment of the status differential, which, even without further reinforcement, represents an unspoken rebuff" (Brown, 2008, p. 378). Therefore, it needs to be stated aloud *by Whitepeople*, who have more *role power* (e.g., teacher, counselor, therapist, and clergy) than those they serve.

Up-Power, Down-Power

Cedar Barstow, whose work centers on the *right use of power*, distinguishes between four types of power: *personal, role, status,* and *collective power* (Barstow & Feldman, 2013). Understanding different types of power is critical to this work. Otherwise, we are liable to misperceive power as based on personality and interpersonal dynamics rather than the effects of conferred power and structural advantages within systems. "Understanding sexuality as a justice issue requires analyzing the power inequities within which persons are socialized as sexual beings" (Ellison, 1996, p. 30).

Personal, Status, Role, and Collective Power

Personal power is the ability of an individual to influence, whereas *role power* is based on the position a person is assigned (e.g., parent, teacher, minister, or supervisor), affecting their ability *to influence. Status power* is culturally conferred, whereby power is granted according to the sociocultural positioning a person is assigned by society (e.g., gender, race, sexuality, and ability). This means that a cisgender man has more status power than a cisgender woman; a cisgender woman has more status power than a transgender woman; a heterosexual person has more status power than a homosexual person; a

Whiteperson has more status power than a Black person, and so on. *Collective power* is the combined power of individuals acting together.

In my roles as a teacher and therapist, I have *up-power* in relation to the *down-power* of students and clients (Barstow & Feldman, 2013). Because I am a *white* therapist, I have up-power status in relation to the down-power status of the Black prospective client I am speaking with about sex therapy. It is important to be aware of this power differential.

Radical Play Act

- **Reflect on your *up-power* status power of whiteness.**
  - **State your up-power status power out loud to your white colleagues, friends, and family.**
  - **Enlist white colleagues, friends, and family to do the same.**
  - **Keep your up-power status power in mind when in conversation with Black people to remain aware of and responsible for your conferred racial privilege.**

Performing Power

According to Barstow (2021), *how* we use role power is further influenced by social (and familial) conditioning, such that role and status power converge. For example, white cisgender men have been conditioned to overuse their role power, whereas white cisgender women have been conditioned to underuse their role power, creating a white feminism that fails to acknowledge and reconcile the up-power status white women have, making white feminism an ineffective steward for the co-liberation of Black women (Schuller, 2021; Dworkin, 1974).

Importantly, *performing white power* is not limited to acts by avowed White-supremacists, such as the Proud Boys and Oath Keepers who stormed the United States Capitol on January 6, 2021, but includes well-intentioned white actor-spectators thinking uncritically.

White Actor-Spectators

Knowing and claiming one's role power and/or status power are essential for cultivating antiracist *skillful means* and becoming an accomplice, rather than actor-spectator (Osler, n.d.). Unlike an actor, whose role is complicit—passive, immobilized, and spectator-like—an accomplice mobilizes to confront White Supremacy directly, including racist structures, policies, and people. Whereas allies educate and disrupt predominantly white spaces, accomplices coordinate with BIPOC leaders, instead of acting in isolation, forging trust based on consent and accountability (Osler, n.d.). Developing accomplice-ship through playmind is the focus of Chapter 7.

White Passivity

As a white contributor to this series, I aim to be an accomplice, remaining open to feedback, especially from my Black colleagues. White sexuality professionals must reckon with our propensity to be passive, performing as white actor-spectators, rather than using our racial privilege to be allies and accomplices. Whitepeople who do not interrogate their whiteness and its impact remain ignorant of—and complicit in—Black-body erasure. Complicity does not mean Whitepeople are *bad* people, but we are too often unhelpful spectator-actors, who confuse intent and impact. Impact trumps intention. Regarding racism and race, Whitepeople are too often anxious, ashamed, avoidant, unaware, with well-meaning intention but uncritical habits of mind that adversely impact Black people. Developing critical habits of mind helps us to move beyond good intentions.

Radical Play Act

- **How do you behave like an actor-spectator when faced with injustice against Black people?**
- **How can you behave like an ally or accomplice instead?**

One Race-Gender-Sex

The social construction of race, gender, and sexuality into discreet (and intersecting) categories makes *one* race, *one* gender, *one* sexual orientation dominant among others in each category, creating the W*hite-cisgender-male-heterosexual* category of privilege. The male–female gender binary is also a dominant classification that marginalizes queer, fluid, trans, non-binary, and "other" gender identities, expressions, and experiences.

Performing Gender

Because caste, according to Wilkerson (2020), is principally racialized, then gendered and sexed, the male–female gender binary reinforces whiteness, so that *performing gender* becomes synonymous with *performing whiteness*. Gender is constructed by and in support of White Supremacy to literally reproduce Whiteculture, historically preventing Black women from being women *politically*. Black feminisms, as discussed in Chapter 3, address this directly through the lived experience of Black women and intersectional feminism.

Butler (1993/2011) characterizes gender as *performative* rather than natural, with femininity and masculinity being socioculturally imposed by heteronormativity. Gender performativity is elucidated in New York City's underground "house" culture of the 1980s, documented in the film *Paris is Burning* (Livingston, 1991). While criticized for its white gaze on Black and

Brown LGBTQ subjects, it depicts mostly BIPOC drag queens consciously "performing" gender and its indelible *whiteness*.

Norm Versus Normal Versus Normative

Socially constructed hierarchal categories establish *cisgender heterosexual whiteness* as a sociocultural *value* rather than norm. While *norm* refers to the statistical frequency by which something occurs, and *normal* the average—or most common—frequency, *normative* (race, gender, sexuality) becomes the moral imperative for how something—or *someone—should be* according to sociocultural expectations, making white heteronormativity America's sexual ethos.

Gender Versus Genre

Because the prospective client sitting across from me is a cisgender heterosexual Black man, one might argue that he has more up-power status power with regard to gender than I do, as a queer-identified person with a feminine aesthetic, but that would be wrong. This is because Black men are typically not perceived as men in our racist society. They are more *genre* than gender, according to Tommy J. Curry (2017), author of *The Man-Not: Race, Class, Genre, and the Dilemmas of Black Manhood*.

Being a Non-being

Given how gender is correlated with biological markers of primary sex characteristics in humans (e.g., penis, scrotum, vulva, vagina), genre underscores how *non-beingness*—in nihilistic rather than spiritual (e.g., Buddhist) terms—negates gender, which relies on the fundamental ascription of *humanness*. This is especially true for Black men, argues Curry (2017), whose racialized *non*-existence prevents them from achieving *white* manhood.

> Because maleness has come to be understood as synonymous with power and patriarchy, and racially codified as white, it has no similar existential content for the Black male, who in an anti-Black world is denied maleness and is ascribed as feminine in relation to white masculinity. If whiteness is masculine in relation to Blackness, then Blackness becomes relationally defined as not masculine and feminine, because it lacks the power of white masculinity. Thus, Black maleness is, in fact, a de-gendered negation of white maleness that is feminine because of its subordinate position to white masculinity, but *not female*, because Black maleness lacks a specific gender coordinate that corresponds to either white maleness or white femaleness—and . . . relates to the white female primarily as rapist.
> (Curry, 2017, p. 6)

MAN-NOT

The Black man I am sitting across from talking with about the prospect of sex therapy is *not* a man, according to Curry (2017). He is a rapist; solely because—*precisely* because—he is codified Black, and thus subhuman, even though he has never raped anyone. It would be ignorant of me to rebut this by saying *but I do not see him this way* (assuaging perhaps my white shame– guilt) when there is ample evidence that White Supremacy does. This is an- other reason why I highlight the sexualized aspect of White Supremacy with the term White-sex Supremacy, because the threat of rape and sexual violence are embedded into our (white) perceptions of sex and sexuality (Brown, 2008; Iantaffi, 2012; Dottolo & Kaschak, 2015).

Radical Play Act

- **Reflect on your humanness in comparison to the culturally assigned *non-humanness* of Black colleagues, friends, and family.**

- **Describe three ways that you assign "non-humanness" to Black people.**

Queering

Now, more than ever, transformational change in the field of human sexuali- ties is needed, including the strategies to get there. White sexuality profes- sionals aspiring toward antiracist ideology and praxis are asking for How-To Manuals. This book is one such attempt. More guide than manual, it *queers* "how-to" as a means to interrogate sexual racism.

In "What is Queer About Sex?: Expanding Sexual Frames in Theory and Practice," Suzanne Iasenza (2010) discusses the need for a queer framework in sex therapy. "Sex is a queer experience for everyone at one time or another. It can be unruly, ecstatic, routine, mysterious, transgressive, confusing, un- predictable, and changeable over the lifespan" (Iasenza, 2010, p. 291). Once a homophobic slur, "queer" has been reclaimed as a gender, sexual, and af- fectional identity by those whose queerness has been marginalized.

Queering as Verb

Queering expands gender and sexual identity (as a noun) to function antago- nistically (as a verb) toward disrupting the status quo (Tilsen, 2021; Iasenza, 2010; Jagose, 1996). Queering as a verb requires that we bend, twist, question, and interrogate normativities. Queering underscores the complexity of sexu- ality, including its fluidity, multidimensionality, incongruity, and paradoxes (Iasenza, 2010). Queering "normalizes our own awkwardness as we challenge our own cherished frames about sexuality and gender" (Iasenza, 2010, p. 292) to which I add *race*.

This queer framework is useful for identifying and dismantling technologies of oppression (e.g., therapy, education) so that the systems responsible for establishing and maintaining sexual racism are interrogated and dismantled. In parallel research, I frame sex and relationship therapy as a *technology of oppression* that is more concerned with *social control* than *social change* given its perpetuation of dominant sexual (and affectional) discourses (Hare-Mustin, 1994; Hook, 2001). While this is not specifically my focus here, I utilize queering as an approach for questioning and destabilizing racist sexual normativities.

In *Queering Your Therapy Practice: Queer Theory, Narrative Therapy, and Imagining New Identities*, Julie Tilsen (2021) considers queer theory to be a requisite compass for wandering "far off the beaten path of normativity" and "also an ideal praxis ally" (p. 5). Utilizing theoretical queering (e.g., feminist theory, queer theory) as a praxis ally is my aim here. Awkwardness, a key feature of both queering and radical play becomes a craft worth honing.

Radical Play

Queering establishes the foundation for radical play, which is serious rather than frivolous, spontaneous not impulsive (Trungpa, 1996/2008). It propels us to explore new ground. Like queering, radical play is disruptive and transgressive. As a contemplatively trained teacher, therapist, and writer, I cannot help but implement radical play in teaching, therapy, and writing, given its capacity to spark alternative ways of knowing through unanticipated and novel insights.

Contextualizing queerness as the basis for purposeful and strategic *radical-play activities* is useful for addressing the *artifice of race*—a made-up yet consequential category with weighty significance that requires panoramic awareness of past, present, and future, addressed in Chapter 1 using regimes of historicity. Here, Radical Play Acts are introduced to consciously engage and disrupt White-sex Supremacy, requiring that we think and act queerly, leaning into our individual and collective discomfort zones.

Unsettling Settlers

Rather than being confined to personal functioning, identity, or drive, sexuality is part and parcel of the historical, cultural, social, and economic context in which it is constructed (Jagose, 1996). Thus, White-sex Supremacy and its myriad discourses construct sexuality to fit within a racialized sexual caste system in which colonizing forces interpolate and assimilate all bodies, especially Black and queer ones. Thus, radical play becomes a vehicle for *unsettling settlers*, by destabilizing the identities, behaviors, and processes responsible for colonizing. Decolonization, broadly framed vis-à-vis sexuality, is the "undoing" of imperialist assumptions (Jaipur Literature Festival, 2020). Yet rather than decolonizing, Whitepeople need to *unsettle* because they were never colonized in the first place. Whitepeople assuming that they can "decolonize" is dismissive of BIPOC and bypasses the oppressive realities Black and Indigenous people experience (R. Kuhn, Personal Communication, March 19, 2021). Whitepeople must build capacity for feeling awkward, unsettled, and unsure. Jack Halberstam (2021) refers to this unsettling process as a *world unmaking*. The practicality of this queerly crafted How-To Guide attempts exactly that: to *unmake* racialized systems of sexual oppression by unsettling Whitepeople. It is a queer practice that Whitepeople can knowingly and willingly engage in to disrupt their complicity in Black-body erasure, with the goal of offering implementable solutions.

Radical Play Act

• On a scale of 0–10, with 0 meaning *not at all* and 10 meaning *100%*, how unsettled are you willing to be in order to confront your whiteness?

• How have you managed your racial discomfort in personal and professional relationships?

   • How will you now?

1   White Supremacy and Sex

Historicity and Home

"People are trapped in history and history is trapped in them" (Baldwin, 1953, p. 119). To examine our entrapment, we utilize historicity. Unlike history, historicity is difficult to whitewash because it emphasizes *quality* not just *facts*. It is based on historical actuality rather than myth. It is the authentic historical account of persons and events. Historicity is equally concerned with *what* has occurred as with *how* knowledge of what has occurred is constructed. This distinction is critical for addressing the racist construction of sex, given that *how* knowledge of history is constructed reveals more than its "facts."

Pontificated by the likes of Hegel, Heidegger, Marcuse, and Ricœur, history and historicity are philosophically Anglo-European and thus biased and flawed. Still, historicity is useful for examining how persons and groups develop according to their historical conditions and *conditioning* within and across time (Hartog, 2015). To understand how sex is *made white*—a primary task here—we must first understand how *whiteness is made*.

In the preface to *Making Whiteness: The Culture of Segregation in the South, 1890–1940*, Grace Elizabeth Hale (1998) acknowledges that whiteness has been efficaciously constructed *without history*, as if existing beyond space, place, and time, writing:

> Central to the meaning of whiteness is a broad, collective American silence. The denial of white as a racial identity, the denial that whiteness has a history, allows the quiet, the blankness, to stand as the norm. This erasure enables many to fuse their absence of racial being with the nation, making whiteness their unspoken but deepest sense of what it means to be an American.
>
> (p. xi)

Hegel similarly engages in the erasure of history when he denies African history, infamously remarking: "Africa is no historical part of the world; it has no movement or development to exhibit" (Hegel, 1899/1956, p. 99). Hegel (1899/1956) based this claim on the complexity of the African character, which for him was "difficult to comprehend" (p. 93), revealing *two Africa's:*

DOI: 10.4324/9781003190035-2

one real, one imagined. Africa as unhistorical is invented, whereas Africa as complex is a matter of fact. This is similar to America's biracial history: "To be American is to be both black and white. Yet to be a modern American has also meant to deny this mixing, our deep biracial genesis" (Hale, 1998, p. 3). Historicity reveals the complex biracial origination story of America's "purity" with references to sex. As with Hegel's Africa, there are *two* sexual narratives: one real, one imagined. One is raced, the other race-neutral. The first is true; the second, false and racist.

Sexuality in America is predicated on race. It is created and maintained by White Supremacy (and its heteronormativity) making sex *white* (Stokes, 2001; Carter, 2007). White-sex is *pure* sex. Focused on intercourse, it is more procreative than pleasurable. Yet according to sex positivity, it is pleasurable too. White-sex is partnered, monogamous, missionary, and orgasmic sex. It is also "vanilla" (i.e., boring and basic) sex. Ironically, vanilla is a very complex flavor in culinary terms. White-sex Supremacy makes sex appear "simple" (like vanilla) by erasing evidence of its *white history*, which in turn erases Black bodies.

Regimes of Awareness

Regimes of historicity, as conceived by François Hartog (2015), serves as a distancing tool that enables societies to reconcile the past, and also the present and future. As a conceptual device, it provides a method for developing *societal awareness* and *accountability* for past injustices with micro- and macro-level consequences (Hartog, 2015).

We experience the present (without critically examining the past) along a *continuum of freedom*, based on our sociocultural locations. From globe-trotting citizens to low-income wage earners, we are emancipated or confined. Regimes of historicity enable the acceptance of responsibility by nation-states for government-sanctioned perpetration, namely acts of oppression including physical and psychological violence that have harmed those who have been systemically subjugated.

I liken regimes of historicity to *regimes of awareness*, whereby the up-power ruling class (in this case, white sexuality professionals) develops awareness of and accountability for past injustices (i.e., White-sex Supremacy). A decisive macro-outcome, for example, would be reparations to African American descendants of chattel slavery. For our purposes, taking collective responsibility would be to perceive sex as it *has been* and *is*— inseparable from White Supremacy. To be accountable for historically racist sexual conditioning, we must first become aware—as individuals certainly, but more importantly as a collective of white sexuality professionals, so as to move the antiracist dial in the right (non-white) direction with effective use of our collective power. The tragedy is that too many among us—white sexuality educators, counselors, and therapists—remain unaware that sex is racialized. Assuming instead, that *White*-sex is *just sex* (but not socially "just") and applies universally to all people. This book aims to reconcile that egregious misunderstanding.

Unsanitizing History

Regimes of historicity serve as "a method of self-awareness in a human community" (Allred, 2017, p. 3) that is underdeveloped in the United States. It is a function similar to what Joy DeGruy (2017) refers to as *unsanitizing history* in *Post Traumatic Slave Syndrome: America's Legacy of Enduring Injury and Healing* (p. 55).

To facilitate individual and collective capacity for accountability and reconciliatory awareness in the field of human sexualities, we must engage the discomfort and untidiness of racism. Using regimes of awareness as a conceptual lens, we will address the unsanitary conditions of White Supremacy and its adverse consequences, namely, the erasure of Black bodies and sexualities.

Traces of Trauma

As we will see, because Blackness is considered a "pollutant" (Delany, 1999) racial sanitization occurs by "civilizing" Blackness, especially when it comes to sexuality (Carter, 2007). White-sex Supremacy encourages Whitepeople (and people of color) to become sexually disciplined—and positive. The work of conscientization, however, requires that we unsanitize ourselves, toward becoming *undone* (Halberstam, 2020, 2021) by accepting responsibility as systemic perpetrators of racialized and sexualized trauma.

> The paradox is that the past is never past. It leaves its memorials as skeletons, traces, and ruins on the landscapes that compel the curious to ask questions and to seek answers. The past inscribes itself in the human body, the memory being the most obvious. Long after memory fades, genealogy and lineage . . . ensures that we do not forget the event of chattel slavery and the illicit mixing of bloods.
>
> (Brown, 2008, p. 385)

Defining White Supremacy

The illicit mixing of bloods relies on the weaponry of racism and rape, demonstrating how whiteness shapes sex and sexuality through the proviso of White Supremacy, broadly defined as the *physical and psychological domination of colonized others*, fostering anti-Blackness that is perversely baked into multicultural agendas and policies (Brown, 2008). More specifically, and for our purposes here:

> White supremacy is a descriptive and useful term to capture the all-encompassing centrality and assumed superiority of people defined and perceived as white and the practices based on this assumption. White supremacy in this context does not refer to individual white people and their individual intentions or actions but to an overarching political, economic, and social system of domination [that shapes sex].
>
> (DiAngelo, 2018, p. 28)

This is why I employ and capitalize the terms: Whitepeople, Whiteworld, and Whiteculture, because Whiteness performs the violence and bodily trauma of White Supremacy.

Importantly, "race is not an intellectual or cognitive exercise, but a political and social construction that leaves scars on our body and nervous system" (Stern, 2021, para. 6). White Supremacy lives in the body (Menakem, 2017) alongside sex. The supremacy of whiteness is inescapable, traumatizing bodies distinctly (Menakem, 2017) depending upon the body's affixed racial caste (Wilkerson, 2020). White Supremacy wields inconceivable violence against Black bodies especially, making anti-Black racism "a visceral experience . . . it dislodges brains, blocks airways, rips muscle, extracts organs, cracks bones, breaks teeth" (Coates, 2015, p. 10). Chattel slavery is an enduring American legacy—an intergenerational epigenetic inheritable trauma (DeGruy, 2017; Jawaid et al., 2018; Lacal & Ventura, 2018; Henriques, 2019). If occurring today, the effects of enslavement would undoubtedly be classified as traumatic stress.

Post-Traumatic Stress Disorder

The *Diagnostic and Statistical Manual of Mental Health Disorders* (DSM-V) (American Psychiatric Association, 2013) has established criteria for post traumatic stress disorder (PTSD) that include exposure to actual or threatened death, serious injury, or sexual violence, paired with unwanted symptoms of intrusion, disassociation, negative thoughts and emotions, and activated physiological arousal (pp. 271–272).

> Traumatic stress is a particular type of stress involving an acute or chronic reaction to shocking and emotionally overwhelming situations generally involving a threat to physical or personal integrity. Clinically, in humans, it exists in the form of acute stress disorder (ASD), which can be classified as *post-traumatic stress disorder* (PTSD) when persisting for more than a month.
>
> (Jawaid, et al., 2018, p. 275)

The ongoing distress adversely impacts functioning and is not attributable to substance use and/or abuse (American Psychiatric Association, 2013). Distress due to White Supremacy meets these criteria: it is significant and prolonged, including across generations.

Post-Traumatic Slave Syndrome

Notably, "traumatic stress . . . has transgenerational effects in mammals" (Jawaid et al., 2018, p. 274), meaning that it manifests in subsequent generations. This is also true for descendants of enslaved African Americans, who themselves were never enslaved, yet experience PTSD. DeGruy (2017) calls this phenomenon *post-traumatic slave syndrome* (PTSS).

> Post Traumatic Slave Syndrome is a condition that exists when a population has experienced multigenerational trauma resulting from centuries of slavery and continues to experience oppression and institutionalized racism today. Added to this condition is a belief (real or imagined) that the benefits of the society in which they live are not accessible to them.
>
> (DeGruy, 2017, p. 105)

White-Body Supremacy

The traumatic physiological impact of White Supremacy is accentuated in the conceptualization of White "body" Supremacy, a term introduced by Resmaa Menakem (2017) in *My Grandmother's Hands: Racialized Trauma and the Pathway to Mending Our Hearts and Bodies*, to underscore the traumatizing effects racial stress has on *all* bodies, specifically Black bodies, white bodies, and police bodies in the United States due to the enduring legacy of chattel slavery, including white ex-officer Derek Chauvin, who on June 25, 2021—1 year and 1 month after his murder of George Floyd—was sentenced to 22.5 years in prison for the trauma of White Supremacy. Chauvin is not simply a bad apple, he is representative of the (intergenerational) fear white cops have of Black men.

> Simply put, white cops are afraid of black men. We don't talk about it, we pretend it doesn't exist, we claim "color blindness," we say white officers treat black men the same way they treat white men. But that's a lie. In fact, the bigger, the darker the black man the greater the fear. The African American community knows this. Hell, most whites know it. Yet, even though it's a central, if not the defining ingredient in the makeup of police racism, white cops won't admit it to themselves, or to others.
>
> (Stamper, 2005, pp. 362–363)

As it has done countless times before to so many other Black bodies, the trauma of White-body Supremacy murdered George Floyd.

Homing Device

The United States is "home" to over three hundred million people of varying ethnicities and races, yet whiteness is its orientation—its *homing device*. Homing device, in this context, is how "we learn what home means" (Ahmed, 2006, p. 9). How we are socialized into coming to understand what matters. It is *how* we belong, or *if* we belong (Phillips, 2020; Yetunde, 2020; Selassie, 2020). Race is a social construction that effectually *stabilizes* or *destabilizes* home. This stabilization–destabilization process is implemented according to the racial affixation of bodies even though race is "an idea not a fact" (Painter, 2010, p. xiv).

The practice of categorizing people according to the made-up category of race permeates historical and current interpretations of bodies, identities, and sexualities, as if race is immutable and traceable back to before its invention, rendering it devoid of history. Ta-Nehisi Coates (2015) underscores that "race is the child of racism, not the father" in a letter to his teenage son in *Between the World and Me*. The genesis of race is racism, not the other way around.

> The process of naming 'the people' has never been a matter of genealogy and physiognomy so much as one of hierarchy. Difference in hue and hair is old. But the belief in the preeminence of hue and hair, the notion that these factors can correctly organize a society and that they signify deeper attributes, which are indelible—this is the new idea at the heart of these new people who have been brought up hopelessly, tragically, deceitfully, to believe that they are white.
>
> (Coates, 2015, p. 7)

Color of Sex

White Supremacy is encoded into our national DNA, present in private moments of reproductive, non-reproductive, pleasurable, solo, and partnered sex, influencing our sexual arousal, desires, fantasies, identities, and behaviors. It also fuels sexual racism, making whiteness the *color of sex*. According to Mason Stokes (2001), who wrote a book with that title. Sexual racism is the sexual rejection of "non-whites" (Stember, 1978). White Supremacy creates an *infrastructure of heterosexual whiteness* because it depends on the literal *reproduction of whiteness* to endure. In this way, heterosexual whiteness is the hegemonic *sexual organizing principle* that impacts *all* sexualities, albeit differently (Stokes, 2001, Carter, 2007).

Radical Play Act

- **What is the color of your sex?**
- **How do you know?**

White-Sex Supremacy

To emphasize the heterosexual whiteness of sex, I employ the term White-*sex* Supremacy. As with White-*body* Supremacy, White-*sex* Supremacy accentuates the physiological and traumatic impact of White Supremacy. This includes how White-supremacist heterosexual sex influences sex-positive discourses historically and today. White-sex Supremacy emphasizes the ongoing sexualization of racialized trauma that includes the historical legacy of rape and threat of rape. White-sex Supremacy functions to critically examine how White Supremacy controls sex, enabling us to address it directly.

Sexual Trauma

As a survivor of childhood sexual trauma, I was young when I learned that rape is not sex—at least not "positive" sex. Rape lacks consent. It is based on power not pleasure. Rape can, however, include physiological arousal for its victims (e.g., nipple erection, orgasm, and ejaculation) (Nagoski, 2015, 2018; Basson, 2000, 2003). This is known as *discordant desire*, where physiological arousal is incongruent with (emotional and psychological) sexual desire that is absent, unclear, and/or confused. As a paraprofessional counselor for a rape crisis team in the 1990s, I learned how rape distorts and weaponizes sex, if not through action by *threat of action*, stoking fear and causing emotional and psychological harm.

Liberal and white sex-positive feminisms distinguish between rape and sex by defining sex as consensual and rape as nonconsensual, insinuating that rape is *not* sex. I want to problematize this distinction, given that what we call "sex" has historical origins in White Supremacy and rape. For example, as financial dependents white women were subject to nonconsensual sex with their husbands in heterosexual marriages. During slavery, slave traders had sex with "fancy" girls, passing them on to their associates to enjoy before selling them. White male and female slaveholders commanded sex *with* slaves and *between* slaves. As mistresses of their households, white women frequently forced their "enslaved property" to have intercourse with one another in hopes of producing offspring and increasing their wealth (Jones-Rogers, 2019). None of these scenarios distinguish between consensual and nonconsensual sex (i.e., rape), which is notable for building regimes of awareness. It is sex, albeit violent sex. This is consistent with the radical feminist view that questions if heterosexual sex (i.e., intercourse) can be consensual for women under patriarchy (Dworkin, 1974, 1987/2006). Referring to nonconsensual sex as something else—like "rape" or "negative" sex—problematically divorces sex from its enduring legacy of White Supremacy. White-sex Supremacy, as we will see in Chapter 6, contains subtle and overt, consensual and nonconsensual, pleasurable and violent sexual discourses—all of which are used to strengthen its power. This is why casual and professional talk of sex, when not explicitly stated otherwise (e.g., Black sexuality), will be considered *White*-sex for our purposes here.

The historical legacy of rape under White Supremacy haunts us today. It is evident in the sexualized white fragility of *Karens*, like Amy Cooper, who falsely claims that a Black male birder in Central Park is attacking her on Memorial Day 2020 (Maslin Nir, 2020). It appears when Karens cross the street to avoid contact with unfamiliar Black men walking their way. It manifests when Black women are referred to as hypersexual jezebels by Whitepeople and the monolithic Black Church (Brown et al., 2013; Lomax, 2018).

It is impossible to remove rape, threat of rape, and the weaponization of sex from White-supremacist discourse, just as it is impossible to remove White Supremacy from sexual discourse, including sex-positive discourse. According to the concept of present absence, detailed in Chapter 3, reframing rape as "negative" still means that traces of rape remain in discursive sexuality. While sex positivity attempts to rid itself of sex negativity by advocating for the *bright side* of sex (including sexual consent and pleasure) rape and threat of rape remain tactical weaponry of White-sex Supremacy, with pillars of *sexual* whiteness (introduced in Chapter 3).

White Standpoint

Talk of sex in *white spaces*—the predominant space of our profession—is conspicuously devoid of race. Not because it is free of racism, but because it evades race. Under the guise of inclusivity, White Supremacy employs the tactic of "colorblindness" (Eng, 2010), which is not an affliction to strive for—given its heritability—which like racism, *misperceives*. In this way, whiteness is a *standpoint*. It is the lens through which Whitepeople perceive themselves, others, and society (Frankenberg, 1997; DiAngelo, 2018) including sex. *White*-sex is synonymous with sex and sexuality, relying on the structural support of White Supremacy to reinforce it through *discourses of normality* (e.g., civilization, erotic love and marriage, sexual health and betterment, sex positivity). *White performativity* (e.g., neurasthenia, white fragility, and blondness) (Beard, 1880, 1881, 1884; Carter, 2007; DiAngelo, 2011, 2018; Rankine, 2019) is the (dis)embodied accompaniment to White-supremacist race-evasive normality discourses.

Pathological Discourse

The task of "white identity is to see oneself as an individual, outside or inno-cent of race—'just human'" (DiAngelo, 2018, p. 27). Whiteness—as a *patho-logical discourse*—manifests as narcissism "whereby a consideration of 'the other' is first and foremost a consideration of 'the self'" (Stokes, 2001, p. 53). It is the mirroring of self-sameness: a narcissistic loop whereby What is White becomes What is Normal (i.e., real, true) because What is White is considered What Should Be. Still:

> Whiteness is not a monolithic discourse, and whites are not a cohesive, ho-mogenous ethnic group. . . . The fact that whiteness is constantly threatened by its own heterogeneity and hybridity reveals it for what it is: an intrinsi-cally pathological discourse which has been constructed to create the fiction of a unitary and homogenous culture and people (that is, essentialist).
>
> (Gabriel, 2000, p. 68)

Vested Interest

This "non-raced" *just human* standpoint insinuates that Whitepeople and their interests are representative of humanity, such that "whiteness has a cash value" (Lipsitz, 1998/2018, p. vii). Whiteness becomes a *possessive invest-ment* to which Whitepeople cling (Lipsitz, 1998/2018). It is the peace-of-mind insurance policy that Whitepeople are doing okay even if they are not. It is proof of betterment—or at least its potential—buoyed by the establishment and maintenance of dominant narratives, including sexual narratives that pro-tect the racial status quo.

> If people perceive whiteness as the only advantage they have, they will cling to it desperately. No matter how dejected, how discouraged, how ag-grieved, or how angry a person may be, whiteness seems to provide a floor below which one cannot fall.
>
> (Lipsitz, 1998/2018, p. 119)

Our possessive investment in whiteness—the proverbial floor below which one cannot fall—is salient in sex. This becomes apparent to me while working with a white thirtysomething cisgender heterosexual male, who sought ther-apy to get his "dick working again" as he described it, with the goal of "fuck-ing some hotties." It was a desire that eluded him, given he could not easily maintain an erection since the contentious breakup with his ex. His physician found no underlying medical condition that might be causing the problem and referred him to sex therapy. It was not until we were a few months into therapy that I considered his sexual challenges might be caused and/or compounded by his vested interest in whiteness.

Well-educated and professionally successful, he complained that he did not "buy" the concept *Black Lives Matter*. Not "buying" it is an apt phrase considering it reflects the *purchase power of whiteness* (Harris, 1993). Curious to know my opinion on BLM, he asked what I thought. I shared what I found to be faulty in the argument that *All Lives Matter*. Unconvinced, he thanked me for my perspective and said he would have to think about it.

During subsequent sessions, he expressed frustration with my stance. I considered it an opportunity to address interpersonal differences, which we had previously established caused him significant anxiety because it made him feel *wrong*, as if he was a bad person. He explained that he had trusted me but was now questioning that. He seemed to be regarding me as yet another woman (albeit queer-identified) who let him down, whom he could not seduce. Already sexually frustrated, he could not fathom a further lowering of his status. When I inquired about the loss and/or grief he might feel if Black lives mattered, he responded: "C'mon. I've got a limp dick, and now my life doesn't fuckin' matter. It's too much, don't you think?"

His retort exemplifies why white Americans invest in whiteness, given its ability to provide power, prestige, opportunity, and resources, including *sexual* power, *sexual* prestige, and *sexual* opportunity. It is the *one* guarantee that when all else (including an erection) fails, making tolerance for failure and discomfort is necessary for antiracist work (Halberstam, 2011).

Mirror of Self-Sameness

Due to racial privilege, Whitepeople are predisposed to seek answers in the mirror of self-sameness, even in sex therapy. The sexual identity they know is the sexual identity they see reflecting back in the mirror, which is typically white and heterosexual.

> The therapy room is like a room lined with mirrors. It reflects back only what is voiced within it. When there is a one-way mirror and reflecting team, they too reflect back what has been provided. If the therapist and family are unaware of marginalized discourses, such as those associated with members of subordinate gender, race, and class groups, those discourses remain outside the mirrored room.
>
> (Hare-Mustin, 1994, p. 22)

If the therapist fails to offer countervailing discourses regarding sex and sexuality, White-supremacist sexual discourses dominate sex therapy (Hare-Mustin, 1994; Iantaffi, 2012). While this project does not focus on sex therapy, it is imperative to understand that where and to whom white individuals go to better understand (even "heal") their sexuality is steeped in White-sex Supremacy, erasing evidence of White Supremacy and Black bodies and Black sexualities as a result.

Notably, "being perceived as white carries more than a mere racial classification; it is a social and institutional status and identity imbued with legal, political, economic, and social rights and privileges that are denied to others" (DiAngelo, 2018, p. 24). We invest in whiteness, like we invest in sex. Our investment in White-sex as Whitepeople enables us to bypass responsibility for the privileges that whiteness affords us, rendering us fragile, reactive, and inert, like my client who did not "buy" BLM. More accurately, whiteness is a centralizing force, framing and controlling social experiences through the structural authority of White Supremacy that is established and maintained through a performative system of *white fragility* (DiAngelo, 2011, 2018).

White Fragility

To fully grasp the concept of white fragility, we must understand that *whiteness* is not a skin color but a legitimizing hierarchical social-organizing framework that invests in and perpetuates its own moral authority (Gabriel, 2000). As such, whiteness is the default for bodies, expression, behavior, and points of view—including all things sexual. Importantly, whiteness is an artifice that can be dismantled. A way to do this is to identify the performative reactivity of white fragility.

According to Robin DiAngelo (2011), a white studies scholar who coined the term, White Fragility is the lowered "ability to tolerate racial stress" (p. 54) by Whitepeople.

> White fragility is a state in which even a minimum amount of racial stress becomes intolerable, triggering a range of defensive moves. These moves include the outward display of emotions such as anger, fear, and guilt, and behaviors such as argumentation, silence, and leaving the stress-inducing situation. These behaviors, in turn, function to reinstate white racial equilibrium.
>
> (p. 54)

Though visible and identifiable, white fragility goes mostly unseen and unacknowledged by those who engage in it. White fragility functions to maintain White Supremacy by avoiding self-reflection, minimizing racism, impeding discussion, hijacking conversation, protecting white privilege, and maintaining white solidarity, to name a few reactionary moves (DiAngelo, 2018). It does this by *feeling* insulted, judged, angry, ashamed, guilty, attacked; *behaving* by crying, withdrawing, arguing, denying, avoiding; and *thinking* such thoughts as "Racism is a personal prejudice," and "I have friends of color, so I am not racist" (DiAngelo, 2018, pp. 119–122).

White fragility also claims to already know. It disagrees and rebuts that the "real oppression" is class, gender, and/or sex—*anything other* than race (DiAngelo, 2018). When teaching, I am often confronted by feminists who challenge the notion that racism trumps sexism in a hierarchical caste system. I explain that the history of white feminisms demonstrates how sexism, while real, adheres to White Supremacy, historically and today, making "non-whiteness" a greater liability than class, gender, and/or sex. Because of this, facilitating the disruption of White-sex Supremacy and its harmful consequences is a significant undertaking. Recognizing the performative aspects of white fragility and its key elements, framed as *pillars of whiteness* (DiAngelo, 2011, 2018), are central to its disruption.

Pillars of Whiteness

DiAngelo (2011, 2018) describes white fragility as occurring within a racist society supported by pillars of whiteness, which she identifies as *miseducation, good–bad binary, segregation, internalized superiority and investment in the racial order, universalism*, and *individualism*. These pillars of whiteness establish the foundation on which white fragility is constructed and maintained.

MISEDUCATION

Miseducation refers to a lack of awareness by Whitepeople regarding the effects of white racial socialization (DiAngelo, 2018). Due to their privileged white standpoint, Whitepeople fail to recognize that we are a raced and sexed citizenry who are socialized to equate "normal" or "healthy" sex and sexuality with (monogamous) heterosexual whiteness (Carter, 2007; Creadick, 2010). Miseducation requires that we interrogate sexual normativities to establish that a diverse and fluid array of sexual behaviors, identities, desires, and expressions is sexually normal (Diamond, 2008).

GOOD–BAD BINARY

The good–bad binary amplifies fears Whitepeople have regarding their racial privilege because Whitepeople want to be regarded as good, not racist (DiAngelo, 2018). Since Whitepeople lack familiarity with and skill in addressing their whiteness, they do not typically confront the systems that substantiate their unearned privilege, nor are they pressured to do so (DiAngelo, 2011, 2018). Because Whitepeople are culturally conditioned to experience comfort, stability, and safety, including mental, emotional, psychic, and physical equilibrium, they are likely to become dysregulated when pushed outside of their racial comfort zone (DiAngelo, 2011, 2018). When Whitepeople are confronted about their whiteness, they often become emotionally dysregulated, which at its extreme can manifest as activated and traumatic fight, flight, and/or freeze responses (Menakem, 2017).

SEGREGATION

Segregation highlights the absence of Black people in the lives of most White-people. Even among liberal and progressive Whitepeople, there is a lack of comradery and friendship with people of color. This absence is costlier than most Whitepeople know, shrinking the zone of proximal development for Whitepeople, who as a result remain developmentally stunted with regard to race (DiAngelo, 2011, 2018; Menakem, 2017).

INTERNALIZED SUPERIORITY AND INVESTMENT
IN THE RACIAL ORDER

Whitepeople's "entitlement to racial comfort" (DiAngelo, 2011, p. 60) includes instances when their worldview is threatened by revelatory hidden frameworks that support unearned status power due to racial privilege (Barstow & Feldman, 2013). Because of this, decentering whiteness may trigger Whitepeople to become defensive by denying white privilege through proclamations of goodness and innocence. This is evident in "white women's tears" (DiAngelo, 2018, Spanierman et al., 2012) and "Karen" maneuvers, whereby white women display irrational sadness, anger, and fear, as a means to manipulate and maintain their up-power position. Because claiming whiteness is often viewed to be complicit in racism, Whitepeople defend against assumptions of badness, causing them to dismiss their white privilege altogether (DiAngelo, 2011, 2018).

UNIVERSALISM

Universality is the belief that a singular monolithic narrative exists. With regard to sex, this includes a socially sanctioned interpretation of sexuality, which most people strive for, namely heteronormative marriage. In actuality, however, only a small fraction of the population achieves the heteronormative ideal of erotic love and marriage, let alone has the economic and communal resources to maintain it (Marzullo, 2011). Universality functions to maintain heteropatriarchal whiteness, as does individualism.

INDIVIDUALISM

Individualism rests on the idea that every person is unique and possesses the ability to bypass processes of socialization in order to achieve their desired goals and/or developmental potential through self-responsibility, individualized effort, and personal virtue. Yet this is untrue, given the reality of unearned sociocultural privilege (DiAngelo, 2011, 2018). Universality and individualism are comparable with the inequalities that established and maintain the philosophy of neoliberalism, namely its "four key concepts . . . autonomy, individualism, responsibility, and universality" (Marzullo, 2011, p. 763). Rather than benign competition, where everyone vies for their fair share, neoliberalism is a strategic performance, designed to reframe human purpose and shift the locus of power to the already enfranchised, namely white males.

White Gaze

Importantly, white fragility illuminates the discomfort Whitepeople experience when whiteness and White Supremacy are broached, including in conversations involving sex among white sexuality professionals. Even as discussions of sex positivity are meant to foreground how alternative sexualities have been oppressed, the *white gaze* (Fanon, 1986) (similar to the *male gaze*) remains the predominant *sexual gaze*, such that socially unacceptable sex and sexualities are often associated with people of color, particularly Black people who are considered lowest caste (Wilkerson, 2020). This includes colonial-derived images of the "Black male rapist" (Curry, 2017), the insatiable "Black Jezebel" (Brown et al., 2013; Lomax, 2018), desexualized Asian men, and exoticized Asian women (Chou & Taylor, 2018).

Still, rarely is the white gaze acknowledged by Whitepeople, even as whiteness persists as the predominant lens through which all bodies are constituted, distorting bodies that do not conform to normative sexual standards centering white cisgender heterosexual desires, identities, and behaviors, thereby subjecting bodies of color to ongoing sexual scrutiny and control.

Sexual Science

Scientific disciplines are key partners in our antiracist efforts but have eugenic origins that must be interrogated. As will be discussed in Chapter 5, the *science of race* and the *science of sex* were established during the same historical period (Laqueur, 1990). As burgeoning scientific disciplines striving for positivist legitimacy, they emulated the natural sciences by adopting taxonomic practices that *classify people*. Thus, the scientific study of sex, known as *sexology*, became a recognized, racialized, and racist scientific discipline.

> It produced new forms of sexual measurement, diagnosis, and classification, along with therapeutic techniques to both define and effect personal sexual fulfillment. These interventions have brought about particular forms of thinking, talking about, and experiencing sex. Although its initiatives have been controversial, sexual science has nonetheless played a major role in the organization and regulation of twentieth-century sexual culture.
> (Irvine, 1990/2005, p. 6)

The new scientific epistemologies for thinking about, talking about, and experiencing sex are unequivocally white. Scientific investments based on classification and objectivity become the mechanisms by which the "sciences" of sex and race are *essentialized*, equating sex and race as fundamental to human "essence." When, in fact, we know otherwise:

> That whiteness is, of course, a delusion, a scientific and cultural fiction, that like all racial identities has no valid foundation in biology or anthropology. Whiteness is, however, a social fact, an identity created and continued with all-too-real consequences for the distribution of wealth, prestige and opportunity.
>
> (Lipsitz, 1998/2018, p. vii)

This brings us to Chapter 2, and the acknowledgment of ghosts.

2   Ghosts in the Kitchen

The Present Absent
of Whiteness

Whiteness claims omniscience. Sees *all*. Knows *all*. When, in fact, it sees and knows very little. Yet its reach is extensive. Its expanse is something we cannot wrap our arms—let alone *minds*—around. But we must try. I do exactly that in preparation for this project: order a relatively small, five-by-eight-inch hardcover book titled *The Image of Whiteness*, filled mostly with photographs with critical commentary on whiteness at the back, to put on the coffee table in our living room. When it arrives, I place it next to the kitschy Knock-on-Wood block puzzle, consisting of 16 four-dimensional wooden blocks arranged in a wooden tray that can be flipped to feature numbers (1 to 10), letters (A to Z), and their accompanying images, which I have prearranged in sexual innuendo to include a mustached leather **B**iker, **C**orn dog, **D**onut, **U**nderpants, **V**inyl record (for mood), and Crazy **8** Ball (for sexual fortunetelling). For the final flip, I add the *racist* depiction of **A**fro, representing blackface and/or cultural appropriation, given that the businessman featured on the upward-facing block appears to be white with shaded skin. In this way, White Supremacy and sex snuggle-up side-by-side on our coffee table as they do in real life.

Scouring our home for objects of whiteness previously, I could not easily find them, as it is everywhere and nowhere at once. "It is not it that we see," says Barthes (1980, p. 6). Whiteness is cleverly constructed to perpetuate and enact "a position of disinterest—abstraction, distance, separation, objectivity" (Dryer as cited in Ho, 2009, p. 37). Whiteness is "everything and nothing, literally overwhelmingly present and yet apparently absent" (Dryer as cited in Ho, 2009, p. 37). Cunning and conniving, whiteness plays tricks. It appears to disappear when it is everywhere. Its tangibility is elusive even as its monolithic structure manifests in daily embodied experiences of Whitepeople *beingwhite*. The *beingness* of whiteness features prominently here.

Present Absence: Plastic Pilgrims

In my search around our home for images of whiteness, I find a few simulacrums and one glaring example: John and Priscilla, circa 1623 *and* 1960, the plastic pilgrims hanging on the wall in our kitchen above the sink, a wedding

DOI: 10.4324/9781003190035-3

gift to my parents from my godmother that I inherited. Colonizer kitsch. John and Priscilla Alden were supposedly the "first" couple to be married in the "new" colony, an absurd and erroneous claim that erases indigenous love, kinship, family, and sex, but is testament to the inescapability of entrenched heterosexual whiteness—the hegemonic standard for *normal* (Carter, 2007; Creadick, 2010; Eng, 2010). John and Priscilla may have been the *first* European White Settler *colonizer couple* to be married on this stolen land, but they certainly were not First People.

Removing their resin replicas from the wall to place on the table next to the blocks of sexual innuendo seemed too conspicuous. In order to simulate the *present absence* of whiteness—its *glaring* invisibility—I wanted something more discreet, which is why I searched for and ordered a picture book on whiteness instead. Mind you, I did not read the book upon its arrival. I wanted to inundate myself and our coffee table with *images of whiteness* that our (white) family and friends could thumb through while flipping blocks of sexual innuendo—becoming curious, perhaps, as to why White Supremacy and sex are cozied-up on our living room table. As with this book, my goal was to initiate a raced and sexed conversation somewhat queerly, because *straight*forwardness is unnervingly and problematically heterosexually white (Felski, 2000).

Radical Play Act

- **Locate *objects of whiteness* around your home. These objects represent violence against and/or erasure of Black and/or Indigenous people.**

  - **Consider how these objects, like Priscilla and John, erase Black and/or indigenous love, sexuality, kinship, coupling, marriage, and Native history preceding colonization.**
  - **How does having objects of whiteness in your home make you feel? Notice any urge to get rid of them. The point is to be with them, not rid yourself of responsibility for their impact.**
  - **Notice if you come up empty. If you are unable to find objects of whiteness in your home, go to a mirror and look who is staring back.**

Absent Presence: Mama and Daddy Neal

The intergenerational trauma of White Supremacy wafts through our home's recycled air, while my partner plays a scratchy rendition of "Strange Fruit" on a simulated phonograph. The haunting lyrics and raspy soulful sounds of Billie Holiday play on repeat as I write these pages, revealing a ghostly *absent presence* of Southern breezes, the scent of magnolia, and poplar trees bearing strange fruit.

Framed

In our home, an 8 × 10 framed photograph of my partner's great-grandparents, Mama and Daddy Neal, born in 1918 and 1916, respectively, are positioned across from John and Priscilla, atop the living room console. Our kitchen table is situated between these two shores: *colonizer* and *colonized*. I belong to the former, my partner to the latter. Together, we sit in the center as family around a circular *gray-blue* (the color of bruising on myriad skin tones) stone table.

According to my partner and his siblings, Mama Neal, who is half-Black, half-Cherokee, chewed snuff, had a mean streak, and used a switch to whip her great-grandchildren. Mama Neal, the story goes, would yell for her great-grandson (my partner) to "fetch a branch off that tree, boy" so she could whip him when he misbehaved, which he (foolishly and respectfully) complied with. She would also yell for him to fetch her cylindrical 16-ounce Jolly Green Giant spit-can, half-full of day-old saliva and snuff. Daddy Neal proudly told his granddaughter, my mother-in-law (who then told me) that he was half-Black and half "darkest Indian" with a tribal name that was hard for her to remember and pronounce—yet another way indigeneity was erased in White-supremacist English-speaking settler culture. Our maternal great-grandparents, Mama and Daddy Neal and Sophie and Joseph Wadas (mine, who immigrated from Poland) never met although they lived in the same historical period albeit in different times (e.g., "colored" vs. non-white whites) via *synchronous nonsynchronicity*, which we will explore in Chapter 4.

Symbiosis

I liken the co-habitation of difference (e.g., Mommy and Daddy Neal alongside Sophie and Joseph Wadas, and my partner and I) to a symbiotic relationship. Generally defined as *living together*, symbiosis is a biological process involving a close and prolonged interaction between two different species, known as *host* and *symbiont* (Kloc, 2020). My partner's great-grandparents and my great-grandparents were considered *different species*, both originating as non-white. His were African, "darkest Indian," and Cherokee, who were socialized Black. Mine were Polish, who were socialized white. White Supremacy and sex have a similar symbiotic relationship, where the "greater" of the two (i.e., host) is "home" to the symbiont. According to symbiosis, home is *on* or *in which* the smaller organism lives.

Even when the symbiont is parasitic (i.e., White Supremacy) and harmful to the host (i.e., sexuality), it does not typically kill the host (or at least not quickly) given its reliance on the host for its existence. These close, interactive, long-term relationships can be distinguished according to three types of symbiosis: *mutualism, commensalism*, and *parasitism* (Kloc, 2020; Dunn et al., 2020).

Mutualism, Commensalism, Parasitism

Mutualism as the name implies is a symbiotic relationship that is mutually beneficial between two organisms. Digestive bacteria in humans, for example, are often thought to be mutually beneficial to symbiont and host (Kloc, 2020; Dunn et al., 2020). *Commensalism*, on the other hand, is a form of symbiosis that benefits one organism with neutral impact on the other, such as the bacteria that eat our dead skin. Parasitism is a close interactive relationship in which the symbiont (i.e., parasite) benefits, whereas the host is harmed. These symbiotic relational features of *benefit–harm, benefit–neutral,* and *benefit–benefit* correspond with historical and current responses to racism: *segregation, assimilation,* and *antiracism,* respectively (Kendi, 2016).

Segregation is based on biological distinction and inferiority to Whitepeople, benefiting Whitepeople and harming BIPOC. Assimilation is the adoption of white cultural traits and/or physical ideals (e.g., blondeness, thinness) (Rankine, 2019; Strings, 2019) that is perceived to be neutral but is harmful to BIPOC. Antiracism acknowledges cultural and physical difference within the framework of equality, struggling to imagine and enact "patterns for relating across our human differences as equals" (Lorde, 1984/2007, p. 115; Kendi, 2016).

In order to (re)conceive and address the effects of White Supremacy within sex-positive discourses, we must subscribe to mutualism's *win-win* approach. Antiracism advocates for symbiosis by interrogating segregationist and assimilationist rhetoric in White-sex Supremacy. While Kendi (2016) argues against wasting time and energy convincing segregationists otherwise, understanding the *win-lose impulse* as it exists in our field is worth exploring, given its ongoing presence in establishing and maintaining White-supremacist sex-positive sexual discourse.

Sexual Discourse

Sexual discourse is not confined to professional speak (and role-power differences) within teaching, counseling, health care, and therapy. Sexual discourse includes this, as well as (seemingly) racially benign and casual references to sexuality that employ sex-positive rhetoric perceived to be "good" and/or helpful (e.g., sexual health, wellness, and betterment).

Discourse, broadly defined, is written and spoken word. It is also the mechanism for how *words create worlds*. Here, sexual discourse is defined as the dynamic social practice that constructs the parameters of our social world, including casual and professional talk of sex, both written and spoken. Discourse is "haunted by nonlogical contradictions and discursive inequalities" (Ramoya, 2016, p. 70) based on the *desire to know*, which Jacques Derrida (1978) refers to as *logocentrism*.

Logocentrism generates a hierarchized system of opposites, and the superior term in these opposites serve to establish their status and thus make the others inferior—for instance, being vs. nothingness, presence vs. absence, immediacy vs. distance, identity vs. difference, speech vs. writing (Derrida, 1976, xviii). The superior terms—being, presence, immediacy, identity, speech—are traditionally favored over their counterparts.

(Ramoya, 2016, p. 69)

This *immediacy of meaning*—our need to know emphatically *now*—serves to bypass detail, nuance, paradox, and contradiction.

Sexual discourses engage in discursive bypass using pathology given the role-power differential of contrived hierarchical categories, such as knower/expert/teacher versus learner/novice/student (Barstow & Feldman, 2013). The inference of pathology establishes a parasitic relationship between sex and White Supremacy, whereby White Supremacy "eats away at" (i.e., distorts) sexuality, making it white. This parasitic relationship is evident in the social construction of *sexual scripts* (Simon & Gagnon, 1969, 1986, 2003; Gagnon & Simon, 1973, Gagnon, 1974/2004).

Sexual Scripts

Developed by sociologists John Gagnon and William Simon (1969, 1973), mavericks in their day, Sexual Script Theory rejected the prevailing *essentialist* (e.g., evolutionary, Freudian) perspective that ascribes sexuality to a *natural drive* based on psychobiological functioning.

Obviously, sexuality has roots in biological processes, but so do many other capacities including many that involve physical and mental competence and vigor. There is, however, abundant evidence that the final states which these capacities attain escape the rigid impress of biology. This independence of biological constraint is rarely claimed for the area of sexuality, but we would like to argue that the sexual is precisely that realm where the sociocultural forms most completely dominate biological influences.

(Simon & Gagnon, 1969, p. 61)

Sexual Script Theory reconceives sexuality as *social* rather than innate (Simon & Gagnon, 1969, 1986, 2003; Gagnon & Simon, 1973, 1974/2004). It characterizes sexuality as embedded within social scripts—inseparable from culture and history—to underscore competing social demands on sexuality, involving *intrapsychic, interpersonal*, and *cultural* scenarios (Gagnon, 1974/2004).

Intrapsychic

Intrapsychic scripts focus on the particularities of an internal dialogue that is mired in social and cultural presuppositions about sex (Gagnon, 1974/2004) that include Whitepeople perceiving others and sex through their white gaze and standpoint (Fanon, 1986; Frankenberg, 1997; DiAngelo, 2018).

Interpersonal

Interpersonal scripts center on everyday expectations of sociosexual interactions (Gagnon, 1974/2004) that include white idealizations of individualism and universalism, beliefs that sexual consent is freely given, and "colorblindness" is the foundation for justice and inclusion.

Cultural

Cultural scripts foreground the narrative ideologies of broad socialized sex roles and sexuality (Gagnon, 1974/2004) that include how whiteness infiltrates sexual discourses focused on civilization, normality, erotic love and marriage, sexual health and betterment, and sex positivity, leading Whitepeople to perceive that "positive" sex is "good" sex and devoid of anti-Black racism, when it is not.

Intrapsychic, interpersonal, and cultural sexual scripts *presence* White Supremacy, meaning White Supremacy—its trauma and fragility—inform our sexual attractions, desires, and behaviors. Therefore, our sexual intimacies, solo and partnered (especially with other Whitepeople) are misperceived as devoid of race, and the adoption of sex positivity bypasses critical examination.

Presence as Being

Within a dualistic framework, *presence* and *absence* are considered opposites, as if one prevails at the other's demise. They appear incapable of occurring at the same time, such that an object or a person—including one's attention—is present or absent but not both. Presence and absence are self-referential and state dependent. According to the *Oxford English Dictionary*, presence is defined as "the fact or condition of being present" whereas absence is defined as "the state of being absent or away." Presence and absence exist within a framework of *beingness*. Therein lies the problem.

Early (white) Greco-Roman philosophers grappled with the concepts of presence and absence and their ontological connection with beingness, interpreted as meaning, or *Truth*. Socrates argued that the absence of the speaker in text (broadly defined) makes it vulnerable to interpretation, creating distance from its origin (i.e., Truth). Plato similarly argued that writing is *representative* of presence because it is *absent* of spoken word.

Compared with presence, absence is lesser, which is not without consequence. Whiteness is the standard-bearer of beingness, whereas non-whiteness is considered the *absence of beingness*—as if it is human counterfeit, like the *fake* 20-dollar bill (representative of White Supremacy) that got George Floyd killed.

Superiority of Presence

Presence is believed to be *superior* to absence, an age-old racist story, given that meaning belongs to the sociocultural meaning-makers in the way definitions belong to those with the role and status power to define (Barstow & Feldman, 2013; Foucault, 1976/1990; Morrison, 1987). For example, a solitary drop of "black blood" renders a person Black (Davis, 2001). Legally, this is the *traceable amount rule* meaning that a *trace of Blackness renders a person Black* (Davis, 2001). Why not instead: *a trace of whiteness renders a person white?* Because the *definers are white*. The White-supremacist *hypodescent rule* assigns racially mixed persons to subordinate caste status (Davis, 2001; Wilkerson, 2020).

Pure Presence

The superiority of presence relies on the notion of *pure presence*, yet no such purity exists, given that everything (e.g., you, me, and sex) is mediated by text (broadly conceived as discourse) (Derrida, 1978). "Deconstruction, thus, moves by exposing these centers as always already contaminated by a loss of presence at the same moment that presence is instituted, making centers and peripheries into nonmonolithic categories of selfsameness but of originary [sic] traces" (Ramoya, 2016, p. 70).

Aristotle affirms representation without superiority of presence by rejecting *purity of being*, arguing instead that *all* texts (again, broadly defined here as discourse) are mediated. This means that objects within categories of suchness (e.g., color, size, texture, and temperament) are universally similar but not the same. In other words, all blue objects are said to possess blue, but not the *same* blue. Each is representative of blue but no pure blueness exists. For our purposes, this means whiteness exists but there is *no pure whiteness*—each display of whiteness is a mere representation of something that does not exist. White fragility is the consequential recognition that representative whiteness at its core is *nothing*. And yet the color of racial and sexual purity is white.

Radical Play Act

• **What is your relationship to sexual purity?**

Presence as Belonging

Presence, simply put, is the *act of existence* which can be more fully (and philosophically) understood using the hyphenated word and activity of *being-in-the-world* (Heidegger, 1962/2008; Dreyfus, 1991). Importantly, being-in-the-world does not merely mean being *inside* of space, place, and time, but *dwelling* within (Heidegger, 1962/2008; Dreyfus, 1991). As a sustained close relationship across splacetime, it is symbiotic. Dwelling, according to Heidegger (1962/2008), possesses familiarity and a *sense of belonging*, which surpasses a state of inclusion.

Absence as Not Belonging

If presence means being-in-the-world, we might assume that absence means *not* being-in-the-world. Absence, however, *is* being-in-the-world but *not belonging* (Phillips, 2020). Absence exists *within* presence rather than separate from it. Absence is always-already present (Derrida, 1978). Presence and absence coexist in the same space, place, and time (i.e., splacetime), but the recognition of absence—particularly for bodies of color—is denied by Whitepeople.

Embodied Absence

> Embodiment refers to our "being-in-the-world" (Young, 1980, p. 142), or how we experience our bodies across time, space, and place (Acker, 1990). Our sense of being-in-the-world is inextricably linked to how others view us, such as the white gaze (Fanon, 1986) through which Black women are often viewed.
>
> (Rabelo et al., 2021, p. 1842)

The same is true for Black sexuality. Embodiment is not just how we experience our bodies but how others perceive our bodies and how we reconcile the misperceptions (Merleau-Ponty, 1945/2012; Rabelo et al., 2021). Because embodiment is mediated through raced and sexed distortions of the settler-colonial white gaze, marginalized bodies become "sites of contestation" (Guy-Shefthall, 1995, p. 359), causing Whitepeople to contend with ghosts (Brown, 2008).

The dilemma lies in the power and privilege of presence. As a mindfulness-based therapist and academic, teaching at a Buddhist-inspired contemplative university, I *care* about presence. Too often, however, presence is prioritized over absence. For example, *presence of mind* is complimented, whereas *absentmindedness* is criticized. What I want to accentuate here is the *absence* in presence, such that *presencing*—the act of becoming present—does not just include but *centers* those who have been made absent by White-sex Supremacy, meaning the sidelined, the unseen, the *othered* (e.g., BIPOC, transgender, lesbian, gay, and queer).

Ghosts in the Kitchen

When margins, the periphery, and between spaces become focalized through awareness practice, as they do in the Five Eye Practices (Dilley, 2015) introduced in Chapter 7, the absent presence of ghosts can be acknowledged.

I reflect on kitchen ghosts while washing dishes, Priscilla and John hovering above my head. The white cisgender heterosexual lovebirds who hung in my parents' kitchen before migrating to mine. Representative of symbolic erasure, these intergenerational pilgrims personify anti-Blackness. It is impossible to look at their images without considering their enslaved property—the "Negro" maidservants, houseboys, and fieldhands who whipped up dinner and were whipped, who would be washing the dishes I am washing.

The erasure of Blackness is evident in both *present absence* and *absent presence*. Absent presence signifies the *ghost-like* presence of not belonging (Brown, 2008). Whereas present absence depicts *omnipresent whiteness*, even as it recedes into the background, appearing invisible. One way it does this is through race-evasive sex-positive discourses.

The ghosts in the kitchen are Black and white, descendants of slaves and slave masters. But the colonizers hold sway over the colonized—evident in white gaze and white standpoint (Fanon, 1967/1986; Frankenberg, 1997) establishing disciplines and discourses in philosophy, psychology, and sexology, centering (white) presence over absence because definitions belong to those with the *power to define* (Morrison, 1987). Toni Morrison's Beloved is an absent presence, murdered by her mother, Sethe, to save her from a life of enslavement. Beloved symbolizes the haunting atrocities of slavery. An *absent presence* throughout the story, Beloved's presence becomes more malicious—more parasitic—wreaking havoc on the story's main characters, Denver, Paul D, and Sethe.

Absent Presence of Rape

According to Brown (2008), multiculturalism—like whiteness—is complicit in substantiating colonial and imperial legacies through the construction of a "cultural mosaic based on celebrations of superficial aspects of diverse cultures" (p. 375). Antiracism must replace multiculturalism, centering the present absence of White Supremacy and the absent presence of victimized BIPOC in our field.

As Brown (2008) attests in *Ghosts in the Canadian Multicultural Machine: A Tale of the Absent Presence of Black People*, "the racial, economic, and sexual collision of Africa, Europe, and the Americas" *literally* made her (p. 377).

> One among millions of colored, mulatto, quadroon, octoroon children, the fruit of Black virgins, Ewe, Ashanti, Twi, Yoruba, Hausa, and Ibo, deflowered by White men. The deflorescence [sic] . . . was no ordinary sexual act of biological maturation. It was the deliberate racialized sexual assault whose purpose was domination and reproductive exploitation.
>
> (Brown, 2008, p. 377)

The *absent presence of rape* is the haunting and enduring legacy of the trans-continental slave trade, which remains largely unacknowledged by Whitepeople in our field today. Presencing must center absence, including the haunting bru-tality of rape, addressing anti-Black violence and sexuality in our field, unset-tling white bodies and White-sex. Despite its negation, the absent person, place, event is always-already present. Africa, for example, is present in Hegel's disa-vowal of it, just like sexual racism is present in our race-evasive field.

Radical Play Act

- **As a white sexuality educator, counselor, therapist, coach, or researcher, reflect on your sense of belonging as a "sex-positive" professional in a predominantly white profession, comprised of Whitepeople who have not critically examined the negative consequences of sexual racism in our field.**

  - **Imagine presuming Black students, clients, and participants *be-long* like you do, when they have *never* belonged to whiteness or our White-supremacist culture and field.**
  - **Imagine the contortions—the professional niceties, pleasantries, courtesies consciously performed just to *appear to belong* to those of the dominant caste—the definers.**
  - **Imagine the respectability politics at play. If you are unfamiliar with the term, *respectability politics* refers to how Black people are expected "to improve their behavior. . . . So white people will see it and reward us. They'll give us a cookie. We'll get cookies! We'll get pats on the head!" (McClerking as cited in Starkey, 2015).**

Theater of Whiteness

In *Camera Lucida: Reflections on Photography*, Roland Barthes (1980) dis-cusses the concept of absence presence in photography, where he concludes that the photograph represents the *not-present presence* (i.e., absent presence) of a person, object, or scene. In the tradition of Plato, Barthes (1980) prioritizes pres-ence to signify thisness—which the photograph, he admits, can *never* be. Barthes (1980) emphasizes that a representation, however keen, cannot equal the original even though its representation conjures up the original through absent presence. The image itself Barthes (1980) explains, is stubborn, weighty, fixed, whereas the *self-itself* (meaning the subject of the photograph) is lithe, fluid, diffuse.

Photographs also reveal the photographer's sociocultural vantage point, and gaze:

It is said that the camera cannot lie, but rarely do we allow it to do anything else, since the camera sees what you point it at: the camera sees what you want it to see. The language of the camera is the language of our dreams.

(Baldwin, 1976/2011, p. 35)

Barthes and Baldwin can help us untangle whiteness and White Supremacy from Whitepeople, such that *representative whiteness*—which Whitepeople enact in a system of White-sex Supremacy—is not synonymous with *beingwhite*, a flagrant and *dysconscious performativity of beingness*. According to Barthes (1980), photography is "tormented by the ghost of Painting" (p. 30). This is similar to the way in which Whitepeople are tormented by *White Supremacy*, making "Painting [and White Supremacy], through its copies and contestations, into the absolute, paternal Reference" (p. 30). Yet for Barthes (1980), Photography is more *Theater* than Painting:

> We know the original relation of the theater and the cult of the Dead: the first actors separated themselves from the community by playing the role of the Dead: to make oneself up was to designate oneself as a body simultaneously living and dead.
>
> (p. 31)

Following this logic, White-sex Supremacy establishes a Theater of Whiteness in which White-supremacist (reproducible) hetero-sex is collectively performed by Whitepeople, which I introduce as sexually based *corporeal theatrics* in Chapter 6.

Studium and Punctum

We can apply Barthes's framework for understanding photography by viewing whiteness as we might a photograph. Barthes (1980) establishes a framework for interpreting photographs by applying *studium* and *punctum*. Studium focuses on "studying" the photograph, which is influenced by sociocultural and political motivations and interpretations of the observer. Because studium is more concerned with liking than loving, its desire is muted. Punctum, on the other hand, represents an unexpected insight—a passionate *prick*—that "rises from the scene, shoots out of it like an arrow, and pierces" (Barthes, 1980, p. 26). The punctum is personally impactful, establishing a felt, unmediated relationship with the absent presence of a photograph: "A photograph's *punctum* is that accident which pricks me (but also bruises me, is poignant to me)" (Barthes, 1980, p. 27).

Barthes (1980) opines that the majority of photographs *do not prick*. "Most provoke only a general and, so to speak, *polite* interest: they have no *punctum* in them: they please or displease me without pricking me: they are invested with no more than studium" (p. 27). Being invested in antiracism with no more than studium is a problem for Whitepeople. With studium we uncover the intentions of the Operator through the role of Spectator. But as the Spectator "I invest them with my *studium* (which is never my delight or my pain)" (Barthes, 1980, p. 28). The blasé attitude of the studium "mobilizes a half desire, a demi-volition; it is the same sort of vague, slippery, irresponsible interest one takes in the people, the entertainments, the books, the clothes one finds 'all right'" (Barthes, 1980, p. 27)

As white sexuality professionals, we can engage in sexual racism with studium or punctum. We can examine our racist and race-evasive inclinations in "sex-positive" discourses by *studying* our possessive investment in whiteness (introduced in Chapter 1). We can also be *pricked* by our complicity in Black-body erasure and our own undoing (Halberstam, 2011, 2020) inspiring us to act.

Radical Play Act

- Consider: What changes the course of your investment? Can you name it out loud?
  - A knee on the neck?
  - A modern-day public lynching?
  - A Black man paying with his life for a counterfeit 20-dollar bill?
  - A young Black girl whose dead Daddy is now her hero?

3 Failure and Freedom, Erasure and Endurance

Shade and light in equal measure are evident in Coates's admission: "The work of writing had always been, for me, the work of enduring failure. It had never occurred to me that one would, too, have to work to endure success" (Coates, 2018, para. 17). While the success Coates is referring to its literary fame, developing endurance to fail *and* succeed is paramount for our purposes too, as it underscores the never-ending slog through life's downs and ups. Without a leaderboard to tally wins and losses, we just keep going—or better yet, as Whitepeople, we learn to *stay;* and as Halberstam (2011) suggests: *fail queerly*, with peculiar optimism.

> Despite or perhaps because of . . . a new kind of optimism is born. Not an optimism that relies on positive thinking as an explanatory engine for social order, nor one that insists upon the bright side at all costs; rather this is a little ray of sunshine that produces shade and light in equal measure and knows that the meaning of one always depends upon the meaning of the other.
>
> (Halberstam, 2011, p. 5)

That light and shade are inextricably bound is often missing from our understanding of sex positivity.

Meaningful Endurance

Meaningful endurance is necessary for strengthening interpersonal capacity for relational and sexual intimacy, according to sexologist David Schnarch (2009), who outlines the value of *staying power* in moments of friction with intimate others—a process he refers to as differentiation—in *Intimacy and Desire: Awaken the Passion in Your Relationship*. Menakem (2017) offers similar guidance for calming our nervous systems in preparation for conversations on race that are emotionally and physiologically activating.

DOI: 10.4324/9781003190035-4

Fallacy of Choice

Rather than "grin and bear it" in the short-term, meaningful endurance is sustained over time because the benefits of ongoing engagement are worth it, intimately and socially. However, *choosing* to endure is a byproduct of whiteness and its privilege. As a Whiteperson I have ample choice, whereas those who lack racial privilege have little to none. Of course, there are critics who argue (through individualism, universality, colorblindness, racial exceptionalism, etc.) that Black people possess choice in a White-supremacist system that stacks the deck against them. However, for those whose bodies have been shaped by the culture their ancestors were forcibly brought to—who Menakem (2020) refers to as *bodies of culture* rather than *bodies of color* to reclaim their humanness—endurance, meaningful or not, is often a matter of survival rather than choice.

Neoliberal Freedom

That success is interwoven with failure is typically tucked away like a dirty little secret we must expose. Whiteculture—bound as it is to neoliberalism—is averse to failure. Based on "freedom" in the context of free-market enterprise, neoliberalism's aim is to *pursue freedom* (i.e., acquiring wealth and property) at all costs, versus *being free*. Being free is a broader social project concerned with justice, equity, diversity, and inclusion, rather than the *freedom of movement* that comes with economic wealth (Eng, 2010; Nelson, 2021). According to economists and legal scholars, choice is "the very definition of (neo)liberal freedom" (Eng, 2010, p. 9). This *capacity for choice* is also fundamental to intimate life, including choosing to marry or have sex (Marzullo, 2011; Eng, 2010).

Sexual Consent

The *ability to choose* is not freely given. Choice, including sexual choice, is constrained by hegemonic power structures and the ruling class (Foucault, 1976/1990). "Neoliberalism's rhetoric of choice works in tandem with a domestic politics of colorblindness precisely to subsume race within a private sphere of family and kinship relations" (Eng, 2010, p. 10). This attempt to "isolate and manage the private as a distinct and rarified zone outside of capitalist relations and racial exploitation" is what Eng (2010) refers to as the *racialization of intimacy*. I posit that sex positivity works similarly, by attempting to characterize sexual consent, sexual pleasure, and the pursuit of sexual wellness (Glickman, 2019) as *based in choice* and exclusively *positive*, as if "positive" sex is somehow immune to White Supremacy rather than a byproduct of it. Neither sex nor positivity can be dislodged from the White-supremacist sociocultural framework in which they reside, illuminating the political context of sex positivity and its *counter-cultural* origins.

White Feminisms

Sex positivity has *traces* of sex negativity within rather than separate from it. In fact, the term "sex-positive" is an outgrowth of the *sex wars* of the 1970s, which took place in academia, where radical and liberal *white* feminisms were at odds with regard to pornography. Those who considered themselves radical feminists, most notably Andrea Dworkin (1974, 1979/1989, 1987/2006), argued that pornography exploited and degraded women by representing them as disempowered victims without sexual agency.

Transgressive Versus Mainstream

In response, an emerging collective of "sex-positive" feminist and queer activists and scholars advocated for female sexual liberation through pornography and "whorish," kinky, and transgressive sexual acts (Queen, 1979/2002). This led to widespread adoption of sex-positive values through sex-positive discourses (Queen, 1979/2002; Glick, 2000; Libby, 2016) in the burgeoning field of sexuality despite its imprecise definition (Glick, 2000; Ivanski & Kohut, 2017). The sex-positive movement that arose amid the (white) feminist wars of the 1970s was political and transgressive, whereas sex positivity presently has entered the mainstream depoliticizing it and reframing it as pleasure-driven sexual optimism.

Always-Already Negative

Invoking the concept of *present absence* discussed in the previous chapter, sex positivity always-already contains sex negativity. Our failure to recognize this as white sexuality educators, counselors, and therapists causes harm. Without critical examination, we falsely believe positivity functions positively *racially*—presuming the *absence* of White Supremacy in sex-positive discourses, rather than its always-already *present absence*, erasing Black sexualities in the process. Efforts to apply a sex-positive framework to address sociopolitical issues focused on justice, diversity, and inclusion though limited exist (Williams et al., 2013) but do not directly focus on how White Supremacy and its sexual discourses shape sex historically and today, which is why critical investigation into White-sex Supremacy matters.

Black Feminisms

Notably, the porn wars (a.k.a. feminist wars, sex wars) pitted *white feminisms* against one another. *Black feminism*, present in first-wave feminism in the nineteenth and twentieth centuries—promoting voting rights and protesting the victimization and sexualization of Black women by Whiteculture—arose more formally in the mid-1970s and 1980s in response to lack of representation and inclusion of Black women and Black sexualities in Western, liberal, middle-class feminisms historically championed by white women (Newman, 1999).

The Combahee River Collective, self-described as a collective of Black feminists committed to fighting racism, classism, sexism, and heterosexism, who began meeting in 1974, understood the interlocking systems of oppression through their lived experience, making it into a movement. In a formal statement issued by the collective, they wrote: "As Black women we see Black feminism as the logical political movement to combat the manifold and simultaneous oppressions that all women of color face" (Combahee River Collective, 1977).

Intersectionality

Likewise, *intersectionality*—a term coined by Kimberlé Crenshaw in 1989—accentuates the manifold and simultaneous oppressions BIPOC face by acknowledging that sociopolitical positionalities (e.g., race, class, and gender) overlap to produce a multiplicity (i.e., web) of intersecting marginalized and/or privileged identities, with emphasis on the former (Taylor, 2010).

Audre Lorde's (1984/2007) reclamation of the erotic from white hegemonic forces situates eroticism within intersectional feminism, where feminists of color, often lesbians from low socioeconomic strata, realized what white feminisms failed to do by directly addressing the needs and concerns of Black women, whose intersectional identities include race, class, gender, and sexuality (Crenshaw, 1989; Epstein, 1999). Intersectional Black feminisms, a radicalization of white feminisms, spread to infuse the Gay Rights Movement, particularly AIDS activism that adopted a collectivist commitment to non-hierarchical leadership (Epstein, 1999).

In the 200-plus years that Black women have been living an intersectional existence in the United States, and more than 30 years since the term was coined, intersectionality remains theoretically useful when applied to praxis (Taylor, 2011). Its looming challenge is to "progress beyond intersectionality as a theoretical paradigm, towards understanding intersectionality as a lived experience" (Taylor, 2011, p. 37). This includes perceiving sexuality as fundamental to "the 'mantra' of race, class and gender" rather than another "spoke on the intersectional wheel" (Taylor et al., 2011, pp. 1–2). Viewing race and sex as inseparable is fundamental to addressing White-sex Supremacy.

Blackness as Hereditary Pollutant

Black feminism establishes that race is always-already present in sex due to the historical impact of slavery. According to Delany (1999), race functions as a *legalized hereditary pollutant* (pp. 268–269). Given that *heredity is impossible* without sex, White-sex Supremacy is always-already present, even in its perceived absence. The inescapable plight that "one drop of black blood" renders a person irreversibly Black makes it so (Davis, 2001).

Pillars of *Sexual* Whiteness

Examined critically, sex positivity—which arose in concert with white Western liberal feminisms—bears eerie resemblance to pillars of whiteness, introduced in Chapter 1, including miseducation, good–bad binary, segregation, internalized superiority and investment in the racial order, universalism, and individualism. Because pillars of whiteness undergird casual and professional discourses of sex positivity, we foreclose on racial diversity, remaining ignorant to the fact that White Supremacy shapes our sexuality. To expose it, I suggest we reconsider the six pillars of whiteness, introduced in Chapter 1, as pillars of *sexual* whiteness:

Most white sexuality professionals remain (1) *miseducated* regarding the historical implications of White Supremacy in the present by believing, for example, that eugenics and scientific racism no longer influence our field (Saini, 2019). We fail to recognize and/or acknowledge that the "sex" we refer to is fundamentally shaped by whiteness. (2) Sex-positivity is framed within the *good-bad binary* (historically and today) making sex-positive "good" and sex-negative "bad" as if sex and sexuality are simplistic rather than complex. We fail to recognize that negativity—and the legacy of sexual racism and rape—is always-already contained in sex-positivity (Millbank, 2012). (3) Sex-positivity does little to alter the *racially segregated* nature of our field. Initiatives focused on racial justice, diversity, equity, and inclusion are still needed in our organizations (e.g., AASECT, SSSS) and garner far more interest among Black professionals than their white counterparts. (4) *Internalized superiority and investment in the racial order* is evident in the tense conversations I have had with many white colleagues, who grow visibly uncomfortable with talk of White Supremacy. Because legitimizing our work as sexuality professionals has itself been difficult, criticizing our field or characterizing white sexual progressives as the crux of the problem can be perceived as unfair, even if true. (5) Lacking clear definition and critical examination (Ivanski & Kohut, 2017), sex-positivity establishes a *universal* monolithic narrative: Sex-positivity is good, sexual consent is possible, sexual pleasure is achievable, and sexual wellness is accessible (Glickman, 2019) without examining the impact of White Supremacy on each of these facets. (6) Sex positivity also rests on *individualism*, which values individuals over the collective and perceives consent as a personal rather than sociopolitical choice. "When we talk about whether the participants of a sexual interaction consented to it, we're really talking about whether they each had the awareness, the capacity, the skills and tools, and the freedom to speak their needs and desires" (Glickman, 2019, p. 22). As further reminder of who gets to choose:

Trump:	"I just start kissing them. It's like a magnet. Just kiss. I don't even wait. And when you're a star they let you do it. You can do anything."
Bush:	"Whatever you want."
Trump:	"Grab them by the pussy. You can do anything." (British Broadcasting Corporation, 2016)

Given that sexual consent is the bedrock of sex positivity, I would add the *mischaracterization of choice and freedom* as a seventh pillar of sexual whiteness, all of which keep White-sex supremacy intact.

Freedom of Choice

"Liberal myths about the 'capacity for liberty' and narratives about the need for 'civilization' serve to subjugate enslaved, indigenous, and colonized peoples, and to obscure the violence of both their separations and their mixtures" (Lowe, 2015, p. 8). These same liberal myths and narratives serve as foundation for *race-evasive* "positive" and "inclusive" sexual discourses (e.g., civilization, normality, erotic love and marriage, and sex positivity) (Carter, 2007; Creadick, 2010; Stephens, 2015, 2018). The colonial processes by which subjects are racially constituted endure through the misleading liberal rhetoric of "freedom" (Lowe, 2015; Nelson, 2021) to align with the kind of sexual liberation and freedom that sex positivity purportedly offers. "Liberal ideas of rights, emancipation, wage labor, and free trade were articulated in and through the shifting classifications that emerged to manage social difference" (Lowe, 2015, p. 9). Sexual choice (i.e., consent) and the "liberatory" promises of sex positivity are inseparable from White Supremacy. Because of this, sex positivity assimilates the BIPOC bodies it purports to care about, effectively *managing* and *erasing* difference, most especially Black sexualities.

Erased

This chapter is *not supposed to be*. It is the result of *failure*, in the form of a colossal mistake. It is due to *nothing*. No-thing, quite literally—what Buddhists might refer to as *emptiness* (i.e., the space from which matter arises) which is more hopeful than I am at this moment and also feels like a cruel cosmic joke.

The Buddhist principle of emptiness distinguishes between nothing and *no-thing*; the latter less desolate, less nihilistic, as if pregnant with possibilities. Yet I feel *emptied* like a deflated balloon. Because nothing of what I have previously written (aside from the preface, introduction, and Chapters 1 and 2) is left. Nothing. Natta. Zilch. Due to exhaustion, I deleted over 6 months of work and more than 125 pages with no way to retrieve them. No Way. Believe me, I have tried: enlisting the help of computer experts with forensic know-how at considerable expense, to retrieve from my hard drive what I mistakenly deleted. All of whom came up empty.

I feel foolish. Like a failure. Because all I can reason is: *Who does this?* Certainly not capable and responsible writers. Concluding that *I am* a failure, who is technologically challenged, now frozen by self-doubt, and ashamed over having made such a careless and rookie mistake. As a seasoned academic, I should know better. *Shame on me.* Oy, this is sounding whitish (i.e., fragile). Let me not languish here. At least not now. Instead, I will refocus on the *freedom of choosing*, which I possess as a Whiteperson. First, by choosing to consciously breathe. A small, yet mighty freedom accessible to those of us who are alive.

Radical Play Act

- **Take three deep breaths, focusing on your *outbreath*. We naturally breathe in. When anxious or stressed, we breathe more shallowly, and our outbreath becomes constricted.**
- **Breathe out, exhaling everything. Notice your diaphragm pulling in. Naturally breathe in. (Repeat two more times.)**

How did I erase 125-plus pages? Blurry-eyed, I created what I thought was a *copy*—which was actually a *shortcut*—for the series editor to read. Because I did not want the series editor to see the mishegosh of my mind, I deleted Chapters 3 through 7 and the references in the shortcut (which I thought was the copy) so I could email a shortened version of my work-in-progress before catching a plane to visit my childhood home early the next morning. In doing so, I erased approximately 35,000 words, more than half of the manuscript in the original document. Worst of all, I did not have a viable backup. It was not saved to the cloud, on Google, a thumb drive, or emailed to anyone, including myself, which I typically do.

I discovered my punch-in-the-gut error when I opened my laptop to return to the project at 30,000-feet midair, on a plane bound to New York from Colorado. Leaving the present to visit the past, in inescapable cramped quarters on a bumpy ride, which the pilot announced was due to tension between two competing storm systems that we were flying between causing static electricity. The irony. The shock I experienced in my body when I realized what I had done might have been confounded by the atmospheric static we were flying through. I could not scream or shake to release the tension, because I was in the company of nearly 200 strangers strapped into a middle seat. I quickly grew anxious, sweaty, and resigned: wondering how—or if—I should/would proceed.

The irony is not lost on me: while writing a book on white complicity in Black-body erasure in the field of human sexualities, I inadvertently *erased* almost everything, including the thinking and writing I felt most proud of, which took concerted time and effort to imagine and create. Poof! Gone.

Epigenetic Inheritance

Losing over 125-plus pages and 6 months of work has been agonizing, though I routinely remind myself that it is *nothing* compared with the losses suffered when *bodies are erased*, an inconsolable loss that is intergenerational: passed down through a process of epigenetic grief and trauma from child, to grandchild, to great-grandchild, and so forth (Lacal & Ventura; Henriques, 2019). It is an erasure that my whiteness allows me to escape, even as I am impacted by the epigenetic inheritance of White Supremacy.

> Many of the times when trauma is thought to have echoed down the generations via epigenetics in humans are linked to the darkest moments in history. Wars, famines, and genocides are all thought to have left an epigenetic mark on the descendants of those who suffered them.
>
> (Henriques, 2019, para. 19)

We are living that dark history now: amid the fissures of a global pandemic; heightened political divisiveness; centuries of racial injustices that appear to be careening toward crescendo; and accelerated climate change that is warming the globe. The list continues.

Due to this heightened state of impending catastrophe and the physical separation required by a global pandemic/endemic, we are more distanced from one another—physically, emotionally, socially—which adversely affects our intimate relationships and adds to our collective stress, especially as our interconnected trauma and grief are underrecognized and unaddressed. The symbiotic nature of our interconnectedness means that helping others helps ourselves, and vice versa.

Racialized Trauma, Racialized Grief

What DeGruy (2017) and Menakem (2017) refer to as *racialized trauma*, passed down from one generation to the next, others liken to *racialized grief* with similar heritability (Muñoz, 1999; Eng, 2010; Eng & Han, 2019), a concept explored in more depth in Chapter 4. Both racialized trauma and racialized grief are critical to our work here. Unlike mourning that involves the cognitive process of remembering (Bridges, 2001, 1979/2004), trauma and grief take up residence in the body. I have had ample experience of mostly sexual trauma in my life, which has coexisted with grief that pulls at my body as if I am a marionette puppet with invisible strings: toyed with at the whim of another, causing me to feel and act out of control in outbursts of rage, self-harm (i.e., hitting my head), and having unprotected sex with multiple strangers.

Radical Play Act

- **Imagine White Supremacy pulling your strings.**
  - **How does it make you *feel*?**
  - **How has it caused you to *act*?**

The meaning I made of my sexual trauma and its accompanying grief indicated that something was *wrong*. Like Barthes's photograph, it signified absent presence: *something not right* was lurking. Due to trauma and grief, I made *myself* wrong, I made *myself* a failure (e.g., *I am* a failure because I inadvertently erased 125-plus pages).

English conflates who we are with our feelings. We say *I am* sad. *I am* angry. *I am* a failure. As if we *are* our feelings. Other languages—Sanskrit, for example—would say something like sadness *has arrived*. Anger *has arrived*. Failure *has arrived*. Reframing feelings as being outside ourselves (i.e., arriving on the scene), instead of being who we are, offers a more spacious perspective, which may be particularly helpful when working with BIPOC who are socialized to think of themselves as fundamentally flawed or "less than" (i.e., bad, wrong). When Whitepeople are unable to establish personal distance from their feelings, they may be more likely to personalize feelings when working with others.

Radical Play Act

- **Rather than experiencing feelings with an ironclad grip, hold them lightly, which is the difference between a closed fist and an open, upward-facing palm. The first is primed to punch; the second is extended in offering.**
- **Consider feeling shame and/or guilt (which Whitepeople frequently feel in race-based conversations).**
  - **Notice thinking: I am ashamed. I am guilty.**
  - **Now think: Shame has arrived. Guilt has arrived.**
  - **Do they feel different? If so, how?**

Visceral Loss

The experience of grief, like trauma, is *visceral* and turns inward. It is the *physiological* pain of loss. Like what happened to me when I learned that my beloved father had died unexpectedly. The news came via a phone call from my cousin near the end of a long teaching weekend. The red light was flickering on my office phone indicating I had a message, but it was Sunday so I decided to wait until Monday to listen. Fifteen minutes later, while in a colleague's office on a break before the end of class, I bolted upright from an inner jolt of urgency (the prick of punctum) that told me I should listen to the message *now*. Upon hearing the news that my father was dead my body convulsed for several minutes: my neck snapped back, my head twisted, my arms flailed, I shook, dropped the phone, and screamed. The swivel chair I was sitting in literally spun around.

Colleagues came running down the hall, stopping abruptly in the doorway when seeing my body spasming, intuitively knowing that I needed space to literally shake the shock out of me. This is what Peter Levine (1997), author of *Waking the Tiger: The Innate Experience to Transform Overwhelming Experiences*, and other somatic-based therapists encourage us to do. Animals instinctively shake in the wild after surviving an attack (Levine, 1997). However, because humans developed a prefrontal cortex and the capacity for reason, our mammalian ability to "shake out" trauma is inhibited. Somatic therapists believe this is why trauma becomes stored (i.e., stuck) in our bodies. There is scientific evidence for this.

Radical Play Act

- **Before continuing to read, take time to shake: Stand and shake your head, shoulders, arms, wrists, fingers, torso, hips, ass, legs, knees, ankles, feet, and toes.**
  - **What do you notice as you shake; after you shake?**
  - **How might you employ shaking as a method to move upset from getting stuck in your body in conversations of White-sex Supremacy?**

Somatic Awareness

Because trauma and loss are visceral, interventions that include *somatic awareness* are essential. Somatic awareness is foundational to our work as white sexuality professionals who encounter sex and sexuality in its embodied and disembodied forms. Enhancing our own somatic awareness is necessary for our racial conscientization as Whitepeople.

For African American bodies—whose ancestors were abducted from Africa and forcibly brought here—loss is daily, due to intergenerational trauma and the day-to-day experience of being Black in White-supremacist culture. Loss is also a lifelong process, involving loss of homeland and loss of belonging—both there *and* here (Phillips, 2020). It is the experience of *displacement* and *dismemberment;* the latter, a word I rarely hear Whitepeople use (until I assign it in a course).

Yet dismemberment lodges in the bodies of the African diaspora, and other bodies of culture, whose lives (and writings) reverberate with the absent presence of their brutalized and enslaved ancestors (e.g., Toni Morrison's *Beloved*).

Dismemberment

Kapil (2001), Glave (2000), and Menakem (2020) address dismemberment in their writing in a manner that many Whitepeople may find unsettling, with a matter-of-factness that is familiar, almost casual. In *The Vertical Interrogation of Strangers*, Bhanu Kapil (2001), an experimental writer and former Naropa University colleague of mine, sought to produce "an honest and swift text, uncensored by guilt or the desire to present an impressive, publishable finish" (p. 6), itself an act of defiance against neoliberal whiteness. Kapil (2001) asked diasporic Indian and Pakistani women to respond to 12 queerly crafted questions in purposely stark and quiet environments to avoid distraction and censored response. One question asks: "Tell me what you know about dismemberment" (p. 9).

A REAL PLACE

When I assign the short story "A Real Place" by Thomas Glave (2000) in courses I teach, many white students become enraged, accusing *How dare you!* Before trigger warnings became commonplace in academia, I resisted warning students about the violent reality they would encounter in the story. I still think it is unwise to warn Whitepeople about the realities of anti-Black violence, as it reinforces their inability to tolerate racial discomfort and truth. Even though "A Real Place" is fiction, the sexual racism (i.e., torture and rape) occurring in the story is taking place somewhere *right now*—in a *real* place, hence the title.

Because white bodies cannot possibly know what Black bodies go through on a daily basis, given the near-constant threat of personal and collective annihilation, our bodies bristle and constrict at the recognition of anti-Black violence that we as Whiteculture are responsible for.

Black bodies know that threat of their dismemberment is due to historical and structural conditions—in *real places*—including within the field of human sexualities. Our niceness, as Whitepeople, is insufficient, as Menakem (2020) attests: "Your niceness is inadequate to deal with the level of brutality that has occurred. Your niceness—I'm glad you're nice to me. But don't attribute that niceness as embodied antiracist practice" (para. 99).

Neither good intentions nor personal responsibility will deconstruct the White-supremacist scaffolding that established and maintains White-sex Supremacy. We must do that with our bodies by becoming individually and collectively embodied through body–mind awareness practices to thoroughly interrogate racist and race-evasive White-supremacist discourses and performativities in our field.

The consequences of passing down racialized trauma are significant, adversely affecting the biology and mental health of subsequent generations of Black people *and* Whitepeople. While epigenetics is in its infancy, it is likened to early research in PTSD, no longer a controversial but widely accepted diagnosis with increasingly effective treatment strategies. Fortunately, with regard to epigenetics and inheritable racialized trauma, "there's a malleability to the system. The die is not cast. For the most part, we are not messed up as a human race, even though trauma abounds in our environment" (Henriques, para. 60).

Keeping On

Despite the mounting pressure of tears pooling in my eyes after erasing six months of writing, I wake up after very little sleep to Keep On—it is what my partner's and my "non-white" ancestors had to do to survive. *Keeping on* is also what I am encouraging you to do: keep on when you feel like giving up, as I did and do. Assuage feelings of failure with curiosity, given that failure is momentary setback (not your identity). When considered queerly, failure can uncover nascent possibilities (Halberstam, 2011).

From Safe to Brave

According to Maslow's (1943) *hierarchy of needs*, physiological needs are the first rung on the ladder to self-actualization. The second rung, safety, is based on emotional and intellectual security and is harder to attain when the color of your skin makes you a target. The physiological need to stay alive supersedes emotional safety, which is why when the white students in my classes state they do not feel safe, I ask if their lives are in danger. I have yet to hear any of them respond affirmatively. My point is not to be flippant or insensitive to their emotional and/or psychological suffering but to clarify whether they are referring to physical or emotional threat, given that research has demonstrated how discomfort gets conflated with *feeling unsafe* in discussions of race and social justice.

Mechanism of Protest

Arao and Clemens (2013) advocate for a rearticulation of *safe space* to *brave space* for precisely this reason, given that when dialogue becomes heated and shifts from polite to provocative, *lack of safety* becomes a *mechanism of protest* for derailing uncomfortable conversations.

White comfort trumps my liberation. Even bodies of culture genuflect to white comfort, because we know, when white people get nervous, people lose their jobs. When white people get nervous, people get hung from trees. When white people get nervous, babies get put in cages.

(Menakem, 2020, para. 37)

Safety Bubbles

Our failure to stay in the heat as Whitepeople effectively erases Black bodies. Our intolerance for racial stress causes us to employ racist tactics based on white fragility, such as *colorblindness* that infers universality and a post-racial state. We buttress ourselves with the psychic equivalent of a barbed-wire fence, or a (literal) *gated* mostly, if not all, white community. We keep ourselves *in* (i.e., safe, secure, and protected) and non-desirables (e.g., BIPOC) *out*. This is the very act of *othering*.

Liberally minded marriage, family, and relationship therapists, whose work focuses on attachment theory often prescribe in-group/out-group havens of safety for their couples (e.g., Tatkin's (2012) "couple bubble") failing to grok the underlying White-supremacist ideology and language (e.g., "primitives, ambassadors, civilized") in their theories. The *intimate we*—which in couples therapy typically refers to two Whitepeople—needs protection from dissimilar others, lest our discomfort gets the best of us. Prioritizing emotional safety in conversations about race stunts our racial development, bypassing the opportunity for differentiation and its perpetual tension between sovereignty and union that most sex therapists actively engage (Schnarch, 2009; Perel, 2006).

I frequently hear sex therapists problematize "couple bubbles" but with regard to consensual nonmonogamy, rather than race. As will be discussed in Chapter 6, the *intimate* (and exclusionary) *"we"* forms the basis of neoliberal coupledom that inflames vigilantism, emboldening the likes of George Zimmerman, the neighborhood-watch volunteer in the gated community of *Retreat at Twins Lake* in Sanford, Florida, who shot and killed 17-year-old Trayvon Martin on February 26, 2012, for the crime of *being Black* while walking home from the convenience store with a pack of Skittles.

Law and Order

Fueled by neoliberal *law-and-order* rhetoric and claims of self-defense, the McCloskey's like Zimmerman brandished a gun. This time in 2020, in an affluent suburb of St. Louis, Missouri on the front lawn of their mansion during a peaceful protest following the murder of George Floyd. The McCloskey's, a white middle-aged couple, believed their *property* was in danger. According to the politics of neoliberalism, the pursuit of freedom in the form of property rights outranks equality for marginalized lives, whose identities are subsumed in "post-racial" rhetoric (Eng, 2010). As we will see, White-sex Supremacy is established on the basis of sexual and racial differences and maintained through the superficiality of diversity and equity programs (Brown, 2008) further reinforced through the *kumbaya* (we are All One) rhetoric of universality.

Zimmerman's acquittal of second-degree murder in Trayvon Martin's death sparked nationwide outrage and protests, prompting the term "Black Lives Matter" to be used for the first time on July 12, 2013, by Alicia Garza, a Black woman and community organizer. The phrase has since become a rallying cry against racial injustice that fomented after the murder of George Floyd, perhaps for the first time sparking (like punctum) a real willingness by Whitepeople to become uncomfortable.

Radical Play Act

- **What is the impact of this linguistic shift from *safe space* to *brave space* for you?**

  - **Where and how is safe space *guaranteed* in your life?**
  - **As a Whiteperson, how is feeling safe synonymous with white privilege?**

Capacity for Discomfort

Building capacity for discomfort (at the level of our nervous systems) is the work Whitepeople must engage in to successfully deal with our white fragility, supplanting it with tolerance for racial stress (DiAngelo, 2011, 2018; Menakem, 2017, 2020). "Bodies of culture are uncomfortable every day. White people have the luxury of not being so" (Menakem, 2020, para. 86). As Whitepeople, we must effort to be with other Whitepeople, in individual and collective discomfort, around discussions of White Supremacy and the making of White-sex—including our active participation in its creation and maintenance, and the consequential erasure of Black bodies.

Discomfort threatens our undoing like a live tripwire waiting for a misstep. Despite our sincerity and commitment to antiracism, our bodies are wired for white fragility (DiAngelo, 2011, 2018; Menakem, 2017). Regardless of our capacity for reason, our bodies fear losing the protection of White Supremacy that secures our privileged status, which is why we react defensively (i.e., arguing, crying, denying, and withdrawing) rather than calmly responding. Due to its tenacious grip on our nervous systems, White Supremacy is hard to tackle, which is why we resort to theatrical performance:

> White tears, white women's tears, can move a nation. They will move people to mobilize. An Indigenous woman's tears ain't gonna move nothing. A Black woman's tears ain't gonna move nothing. . . . This idea of being able to land this race question in a way where white people are uncomfortable is a fallacy. It's performance art.
>
> (Menakem, 2020, para. 86)

This is why antiracist work for Whitepeople must include our bodies and nervous systems—which brace in discomfort, as the physiological effects of anticipatory failure and fear take hold. Whitepeople are not immune to racial trauma. We experience it in our bodies through generations, just like bodies of culture, given that all bodies are impacted by White Supremacy, albeit differently (Menakem, 2017). According to epigenetics, "it is not that fear is being passed down the generations—it is that fear . . . in one generation leads to sensitivity . . . in the next" (Henriques, 2019, para. 29). The sensitivity that is white fragility, spurred on by the trauma of White-body Supremacy, is not a legacy we want to pass on to our great-great-great-grandchildren.

Somatic Dissonance and Failure

It is impossible to avoid failure. Discomfort and failure are bound together. Failure and discomfort are the foundation, route, and goal: the ground, path, and fruition. I routinely counsel clients seeking help with relational challenges to be conscious of their goals, so as not to set unrealistic expectations. There is no relational *nirvana*, no state of perfection. There are only fallible selves in relationship with fallible others, whose bodies feel immense discomfort. It is what I refer to as *somatic dissonance* and define as intra-bodily tension in heated moments of intersubjective conflict that frequently register as disconnection and *failure*. Remember, we will fail, but we are not failure personified.

Staying Power

Developmentally, we have leading and trailing edges (Garvey Berger, 2012), areas in which our capacity for complexity (including somatic dissonance) is well developed, and areas in which it is not. Whiteness serves as a psychological bypass, keeping Whitepeople from having to develop their relational potential. We avoid doing the cultural and developmental work necessary to effect change, simply because we can. In fact, too often, Whitepeople approach Black people by attempting to:

> whitesplain about race and what should be happening, that's why people of color go . . . Like, "Are you out of your mind?" People of culture like, "How do you even get the temerity to try and explain that to me?" And so that's the piece that there's a level of immaturity.
> (Menakem, 2020, para. 135)

Desire Differential

Whitepeople are underdeveloped in the capacity to tolerate racial stress (DiAngelo, 2011, 2018). We are uncomfortable to the point of leaving. We react instead of respond. We aggress, vacate, and collapse (i.e., fight, flee, and freeze). The influence of Schnarch and his proposed *Four Points of Balance* is apparent throughout *My Grandmother's Hands*, and in Menakem's work more broadly, who studied with Schnarch. It is the intimate work of differentiation, which Esther Perel (2006) also references (e.g., in her book *Mating in Captivity*), where we learn how to soothe ourselves, rather than rely on soothing from others. It is not that we cannot (or should not) be soothed by others, rather that we, as adults, can develop the capacity to soothe ourselves. This is particularly applicable in intimate sexual relationships, where partners are struggling with desire differential, as my clients frequently are, where one partner has more (or less) desire for sex than the other (Schnarch, 2009). This is also true of social interactions between Whitepeople and Black people, where Whitepeople are in the low desire position based on their privileged racial status. Due to the *law of lesser intent*, the person in the lower desire position controls the sex—in this case, sociocultural political sex, and the making of White-sex Supremacy, also evident in the insufficient knowledge Whitepeople have about Black sexualities, pointing again to the need for this book series.

Points of Balance

The developmental task for us as Whitepeople becomes focused on effectively soothing ourselves in community with other Whitepeople *and* bodies of culture, amid tense conversations about White-sex Supremacy. This necessary work can benefit from developing capacities that Schnarch (2009) refers to as *The Four Points of Balance*, which help maintain our equanimity in the face of interpersonal challenge. These include (1) *Solid and Flexible Self*, the capacity to clarify who we are and what matters to us, while remaining open to being influenced by others, enabling us to claim our whiteness and be responsible for its impact on bodies of culture; (2) *Quiet Mind, Calm Heart*, the capacity to self-regulate and self-soothe our anxieties, which helps increase our tolerance for racial stress; (3) *Grounded Responding*, the capacity to remain centered and engaged when a close other is upset, especially during conversations about race, allowing us to stay when we want to flee; and (4) *Meaningful Endurance*, which I referenced at the onset of this chapter, as the capacity to "tolerate discomfort for the sake of growth" by critically examining our racial privilege (Schnarch, 2009, p. 74).

Radical Play Act

- What is your relationship to the Four Points of Balance from the perspective of White Supremacy?
- What are your leading and trailing developmental edges?
- How do you need to grow?

As professionals in the field of sexuality, it is our responsibility to grow our trailing edges. First, by learning how to *stay:* feeling uncomfortable and staying with *ourselves;* feeling uncomfortable and staying with *others.* Feeling angry, hurt, frightened, awkward, resistant, and/or misunderstood, and *staying* nevertheless is a skill that bodies of culture have had to perfect in a nation built by White Supremacy, because *not staying* amid discomfort is life-threatening.

Cultivating Willingness

Building capacity for discomfort includes being willing when you do not want to; to see if your *willingness* turns into *want;* to continue even if it does not; to remember that your *meta-want* is bigger than your momentary *not-want* (e.g., to be antiracist in *actuality* not just *theory*); and to keep on when you have the choice to give up. Because not all people do, particularly those whose bodies and lives can be easily erased. I have learned up close in intimate relationships with Black family, friends, and colleagues what not having choice looks like, when the very fact of your existence depends upon you *not* giving up. This, on a daily basis.

Although the work here is ours to do as Whitepeople, the *real* benefit (if done well) will be for our Black colleagues, clients, patients, and students, most of whom we will never meet. And here *I am* wanting to quit—a desire that I am keenly aware of is a byproduct of my white privilege, functioning as another form of Black-body erasure. Unsurprisingly, my desire to quit is being supported by "well-meaning" white colleagues, who are empathetic to my wanting to give up. *It's okay, Carole. Quit if you want to. There will be other opportunities.* On the other hand, my partner is furious at me for even considering it, and now we are fighting. While not in this field, he is a Black man who recognizes what is at stake. More importantly, giving up has never been an option for him.

It is not lost on me that the reflective prompt at the end of Chapter 2 (now, as if prophetically) asks: *What changes the course of our investment?* Is it the knee on the neck of a Black man by a white police officer sworn to protect, who in a public display of a modern-day lynching, murders George Floyd? Or is it the recognition that the last words left after hitting "delete" on my computer, refer to a young Black girl pining for Daddy? Her Hero. That is what does it for me, catching in my throat causing tears to finally flow.

Fail Well, Fail Again

The desire of Gianna Floyd (whose first name she shares with my stepdaughter) to play with Daddy again is what simultaneously breaks and builds me back up. Because of Black daughters named Gianna, I am up after three hours of fitful sleep, keeping on, (re)writing. I begin by retitling Chapter 3 (i.e., Failure and Freedom, Erasure and Endurance) now that I better understand the racialized implications of failure, freedom, erasure, and endurance. I want to escape (out of) Now—into the future or a glorified past—where my Work is Done, rather than being stuck in the incompleteness of starting all over, which is akin is our task here. Starting over, and over, and over. Again, and again, and again. Failing. Failing again.

I reference Halberstam (2011) at the start of this chapter because I needed a sliver of sunshine, with equal parts light and shade. I have always encouraged my students to consider this unlikely combination in preparing for "success" but I am struggling to take my own advice. The adage is true: *Easier said than done*.

Queer Art and Failure

My partner will tell you that he is *black-and-white* (not referring to race), whereas I am *gray*. He likes answers, I prefer questions. He values efficiency and getting to the point. I like dillydallying (e.g., flaneuring, introduced in Chapter 7) and considering *all* sides. My penchant for grayness, however, evaporates when I am scared (e.g., of failing or being judged) which is what I am feeling currently.

What I need to begin rewriting 125 deleted pages is the vivid reminder of epic failure. In the *Queer Art of Failure*, Halberstam (2011) references Olive, the main character in the movie *Little Miss Sunshine*, who as a spirited albeit unlikely beauty contestant gyrates and stripteases to the song Superfreak. Halberstam (2011) uses this scene to formulate a new kind of optimism that repurposes negativity by reimagining "success" outside the confines of neoliberal tyranny.

Olive reminds me of my own budding optimism at the age of 9, when I stepped out of formation in a tap recital with other young performers, vigorously swinging my hips and red hair, with a buck-toothed grin in a face full of freckles, oozing confidence that was not reliant on the artifice of positive thinking or perceiving the bright side at all costs. I simply stood in the spotlight and shimmied. Out of formation and offbeat. As Whitepeople, we need to strengthen our capacity for queer artistry and failure, shimmying out of formation and offbeat (without cultural appropriation) by mentally and physically *flaneuring* so as to loosen our disciplined proclivities for white success and its gilded optimism, beginning by understanding how white positivity intersects with time.

4 Positivity and Time

Positivity has a way of propelling us forward—away from the past, out of the present, and *Back to the Future* (Cooper, 2016). Like the street I grew up on in Whitesboro. By returning to the future (time and again), we shirk responsibility for our racist past *and* present. Often, with faulty optimistic rationale: *There's been progress. Can we just move on?* Moving *back* to the future emphasizes the cooption of positivity and time by whiteness. Whitepeople, for example, routinely dismisses or avoid what is occurring in the present, often with exasperation: *Talk of race/racism, again?* Notice the subtle (or not so subtle) implication of time: *Aren't we passed this, already?* Like my Republican cousin, who after Barrack Obama was first elected president in 2008, said *Well, at least the Democrats can't say we're racist anymore.* With this statement, he attempts to push time forward (away from Now) using racial exceptionalism to suggest something *positive*—that we live in post-racist society, which he would say is a value of his (that I do not dispute). The problem is, he believes our post-racist society is occurring in the present, solely because a Black man was elected president. We know how that turned out: White Supremacy elected Trump.

There is also an inference to speed, so that time will move quickly: *Can't we just hurry up?* Velocity is the direction and momentum with which something moves through splacetime. Whitepeople move *forward fast*.

Radical Play Act

- **How do you as a Whiteperson:**
    - **Disregard the past?**
    - **Pop out of the present?**
    - **Project into the future?**
- **What is your relationship to speed?**
    - **How is it fueled by White Supremacy?**

As sexuality professionals who aspire to antiracist practice, reflecting on our relationship with time is critical. Time is political. It is also gendered,

DOI: 10.4324/9781003190035-5

sexed, and raced (Felski, 2000; Halberstam, 2005; Freeman, 2010; Cooper, 2016). Although we typically do not recognize or reflect upon this, it is *time* (tongue-in-cheek) that we do. Otherwise, we are complicit with *white-time* (Cooper, 2016), as we are with white (neoliberal) freedom, which we have learned is more concerned with acquiring wealth than ensuring equality (Eng, 2010, Coates, 2018, Nelson, 2021).

Temporality

Temporality is the relationship we have with time. We exist within time in a way that binds us (Felski, 2000). Like racial privilege, Whitepeople own time, assigning it cash value (Felski, 2000; Freeman, 2010). Depending on our social locations (i.e., race, gender, and sexual orientation), we live inside and/ or outside of standardized time, given how conventional time is orchestrated.

Relative and Absolute Time

Time constructs a framework for organizing daily experiences, the course of a lifetime, and the conceptualization of history and myth (Felski, 2000). Like heterosexual whiteness, time is an organizing principle. It is an instrument of privilege and power (Felski, 2000; Halberstam, 2005; Freeman, 2010). The relationship of time to other variables, including space, place, and bodies, is personally *and* collectively experienced. There is *relative* (personal) experience of time, and *absolute* (collective) experience of time. Notably, absolute (i.e., universal) time needs to be *mutually agreed upon* (Thorne, 2013). We accept white time, gendered time, and sexed time unconsciously and/or dysconsciously, by failing to question time's sociopolitical construction and thus its validity (Cooper, 2016, Halberstam, 2005; Freeman, 2010).

Spacetime

Physicists, on the other hand, agree to *consciously define time* in a manner whereby the laws of physics appear simple, making spacetime universal and our movement through it (e.g., the speed of light) the same measurement for everyone (Thorne, 2013; Hartog, 2015). This forms the basis of hegemonic time that is scientific (Saini, 2019). Hegemony, or the dominant influential control of one entity over another, is not absent from time.

   Time as an organizing principle is conventionally and collectively conceived in North America to be *linear* and *circular*. The thrusting forward of time coupled with its cyclical seasons causes it to be perceived heteronormatively, although it can be queerly (re)perceived too (Halberstam, 2005; Freeman, 2010).

Modern Versus Postmodern

Modern and postmodern temporalities engage history and experience through heteronormative and queer frameworks. Modern history is typified by a heteronormative—sequential and horizontal—evolution that is universally explained, "truthfully" rendered, and finite in its duration (Felski, 2000). Contrarily, postmodernism shatters the realm of a singular sequential history by queering it—insinuating a *vertical* dimension in which to experience multiple and concurrent temporalities (Felski, 2000; Scharmer, 2019).

The simultaneity of same and different histories converging in splacetime—as George Floyd and Derek Chauvin, and the Coopers do on May 25, 2020—is demonstrated in the dialectic framework of synchronous nonsynchronicity (Bloch, 1932/1977, 1935/1991) introduced in Chapter 2, whereby people live during the same historical period yet have vastly different experiences of that time depending on their social locations. Here, time becomes complex, beckoning a more vertical interrogation.

Because queer time (and bodies) do not conform to conventional sociocultural frameworks with predetermined sequences—of desires, behaviors, and outcomes—"sex may unbind selves and meanings" (Freeman, 2010, p. xxi). The process of unbinding self from sexual expectations requires that psychosexual development center complexity. As we will explore, queer temporality may provide the language, conceptualization, and practice needed to shift us from a *fixed mindset* (of whiteness) to a more complex *growth mindset* (Dweck, 2006) (of antiracism) making the impact of White-sex Supremacy conscious, such that racial diversity, inclusion, and justice more readily occurs in our field.

Heteronormative Time

Conventional time, including its sexual (i.e., reproductive) life, is structured heteronormatively. It operates both linearly and cyclically to correspond with hegemonic expectations based on production and *re*production, including work, marriage, sex, offspring, death, and descendants—a cycle that repeats through time, ensuring legacy. It is white bourgeoisie (i.e., middle and upper class) "family" time centered around normative practices of "healthy" childrearing (Halberstam, 2005).

Chrononormativity is the institutionalization and somatization of time in a society and its people, creating the illusion of "natural" time as being sequential for people with racial, sexual, and economic privilege, such as those who have standard (9–5) work hours, and adhere to scheduled routines (Freeman, 2010). Chrononormativity supports capitalist values and those who own society's means of production and wealth. An example of privileged time is the "50-minute (therapeutic) hour" that allows therapists to take 10-minute breaks between sessions for making notes, going to the bathroom, and so on, all on the *client's dime*. Time is a function of privilege, power, and wealth. Notice the economics of time in the euphemisms: *Don't waste my time. Make it worth my while.*

Radical Play Act

• **If you are a white sex therapist using a 50-minute hour, are you willing to change to a 60-minute hour, at least for clients of color?**

  • **If not, why not?**

Gendered Time

Chronobiopolitics arranges time according to the gender binary, creating distinct "male" and "female" spheres of time for men and women, accentuating distinct "masculine" versus "feminine" temporalities, or relationships with and to time.

PHALLOCENTRIC TIME

In its *linear* form, time is considered phallocentric. Here, time is organized efficiently. It is focused on industry, productivity, achievement, and quickness. Phallocentric time values the "masculine" characteristics of assertiveness, aggression, and speed (Felski, 2000). Its function is to be efficiently productive.

GYNOCENTRIC TIME

In its *circular* form, time is considered gynocentric, or recurrent and reproductive. Here, time is organized cyclically (i.e., seasonally) to align with nature and reproduction (e.g., phases of the moon, menstruation) and agrarian cycles (e.g., planting, birthing, harvesting, dying). Here, time moves slowly, valuing "feminine" qualities of emoting and relating over efficiency, productivity, and speed (Felski, 2000).

Relationship science employs the terms "instrumentality" and "expressiveness" to replace gendered ("masculine" and "feminine") qualities and characteristics (Bem, 1993), paving the way for how time can be reimagined and spent as functions of doing *and* being, which manifest in queer time.

QUEER TIME

Because queerness moves beyond binary gendered and sexed characteristics, queer time is neither linear nor cyclical, rather circuitous.

Queer uses of time and space develop, at least in part, in opposition to the institution of family, heterosexuality, and reproduction. They also develop according to other logics of location, movement, and identification. If we try to think about queerness as an outcome of strange temporalities,

imaginative life schedules, and eccentric economic practices, we detach queerness from sexual identity and come closer to understanding Foucault's comment in "Friendship as a Way of Live" that "homosexuality threatens people as a 'way of life' rather than as a way of having sex" (p. 310).
(Halberstam, 2005, p. 1).

Non-sequential queer time disrupts chrononormativity, threatening the capitalistic stability of White Supremacy. Queer time has no particular order or speed. Bodies in queer time: stop, jump, stomp, sniff, howl, skip, snort, shimmy, scream, start, roll, pause, lay, flop, hop, fall and so on, as I have seen occur in my classes when I introduce chronobiopolitics and instruct students to move: first *phallocentrically*, then *gynocentrically*, and finally *queerly*, to experience how their bodies move differently within different conceptualizations of splacetime. I do this to illuminate how our bodies move according to normative—meaning phallocentric, gynocentric, and white—versus queer and "non-white" temporalities.

Radical Play Act

- Notice how time *moves* your body:

  - Practice moving phallocentrically: Determined, fast, linearly. What do you experience in your body?
  - Practice moving gynocentrically: Relationally, slow, circularly. What do you experience in your body?
  - Practice moving queerly: Curiously, questioningly, unknowingly. What do you experience in your body?

- How do the various expressions of time compare to each other in your experience?

Civilized Time

Queer temporality deconstructs normative assumptions about how time is organized, moving toward fluidity, formlessness, and chaos, with "the potential for a life unscripted" (Halberstam, 2005, p. 2). This *potential for a life unscripted* is the antithesis of time that has been colonized, useful for disrupting White-sex Supremacy by rejecting notions of time and sexuality that are *civilized*.

Chaos and Eros

"The arrival of chaos should be regarded as extremely good news," Chögyam Trungpa, Naropa's founder, was fond of saying, given how chaos prompts us to stabilize ourselves—like a vector in the wind—amid chaos and uncertainty.

According to Greek mythology, Eros was a primeval god, *born of chaos* (alongside Aphrodite) in the wake of seafoam when the god Cronus cut off Uranus's genitals and threw them into the sea. As a primeval god, Eros represented the vastness of creation and the emptiness of the universe. Yet time reveals how the origination story of Eros has been altered. Rather than being born of chaos—and beyond parentage—Eros becomes the *civilized son* of Aphrodite & Zeus (King of Gods), of Aphrodite & Ares (God of War and Battle), and of Aphrodite & Hermes (Divine Messenger of the Gods). Patriarchal heteronormativity remakes Eros into a Roman son, increasingly human, boyish, and civilized, until he manifests as the white cherubic boy known as Cupid. This demonstrates how time colonizes sexual chaos and power by *civilizing Eros*.

Sex Time

Similarly, sexual activity and pleasure are conventionally constructed through heterosexual scripting—beginning with foreplay, continuing with coitus, and culminating in orgasm. This *reproduceable* sequence of *sex time* relies on phallocentric and gynocentric temporality that is linear and cyclical, rather than fluid, chaotic, and queer (Halberstam, 2005; Freeman, 2010). Queer time allows for the disruption of conventional time, which Whitepeople own (Cooper, 2016).

White Time

"If time had a race," states cultural theorist Brittney Cooper (2016), "it would be white" (1:06–1:13). Conventional time thrusts forward *phallocentrically*—away from the past and present, and from taking responsibility for either. White fragility, on the other hand, operates gynocentrically—cycling back, time and again, to emotional overwhelm (Freeman, 2010), such that our actions become defensive. Phallocentric time and gynocentric time shape white time.

Given their up-power status, Whitepeople dictate the timeframe of our work day (e.g., 9–5), the cost of our time (e.g., hourly wage), and the pace of social inclusion (e.g., voting rights legislation) (Cooper, 2016). Whitepeople do, in fact, *own time* and its narrative, scripting our past, present, and future. For example, white time erases Africa's historical contributions to American and world history (Camara, 2005) and relegates eugenicist science to the annals of history rather than acknowledging its presence in scientific (sexuality) research today (Saini, 2019).

White time reproduces, literally: "The wretched of the earth do not decide to become extinct, they resolve, on the contrary, to multiply: life is their only weapon against life, life is all that they have" (Baldwin, 1976/2011, p. 16). Baldwin (1976/2011) goes on to say, "this is why the dispossessed and starving will never be convinced (though some may be coerced) by the population-control programs of the civilized" (p. 16), placing sex time under White-supremacist control. Civilization discourse, as we will explore in Chapter 6, characterizes reproduction as the noble duty of white women to reproduce white heirs for white civilization.

Fast Forward

White time moves forward, without looking back. It fails to take responsibility for past injustices. If we cannot turn back time to relive it, at least we can *study* the past (i.e., studium) so as to witness and address its atrocities, including how history manifests currently through absent presence with queer potential for a life unscripted (i.e., punctum).

GEORGE FLOYD

We cannot, for example, turn back time to prevent George Floyd's public execution, but we can study the video of the horror unfolding to learn that time has changed. In this case, *lengthened*.

In the opening statement of the criminal trial against ex-officer Chauvin, who was found guilty on all accounts, we learn that murdering George Floyd took nine minutes and 29 seconds, one minute and 23 seconds longer than originally thought (Levenson, 2021). Prosecuting attorney Jerry Blackwell divided time into three segments to reperceive history more accurately. By doing so, Blackwell learned that for the first four minutes and 45 seconds, George Floyd pleaded for help. He flailed and seized for the next 53 seconds. And in the final three minutes and 51 seconds, George Floyd was unresponsive (Levenson, 2021). This piercing recognition (i.e., punctum) ignites outrage, knowing that the agony of dying for George Floyd's was further prolonged.

Synchronous Nonsynchronicity

The simultaneity of same and different histories converging is demonstrated in the dialectic framework of *synchronous nonsynchronicity*, initially conceived by Ernst Bloch (1935/1991) to explain how groups of people living during the same historical period of time have different experiences of that time. Rather than the oversimplification that is white time, time becomes *simultaneously* synchronous and nonsynchronous, making it queer and complex (Halberstam, 2005; Freeman, 2010):

> Not all people exist in the same Now. They do so only externally, by virtue of the fact that they may all be seen today. But that does not mean that they are living at the same time with others. Rather, they carry earlier things with them, things which are intricately involved. One has one's times according to where one stands corporeally, above all in terms of classes.
>
> (Bloch, 1932/1977, p. 22)

Different Nows

I would amend the last word in the last sentence, from "classes" to "races," given that Black people and Whitepeople do not exist in the same Now.

Together and separately, according to racial casting, we exist in raced splace-time that operates on the basis of White-sex Supremacy, including its pillars of sexual whiteness, with contrasting intrapsychic, interpersonal, and cultural scripts (Gagnon, 1974/2004; Gagnon & Simon, 1973) for those who are Black and those who are white.

Central Park Ramble

There are moments—like in the Ramble in Central Park where the Coopers meet—that expose distinct Nows, enabling us to (re)perceive with greater accuracy as historicity instructs, the historical effects of White-sex Supremacy manifesting in the present (i.e., the piercing of punctum). This is what I observed when I watched the news and replayed the video of the Coopers meeting in the Ramble: theatrical White-sex Supremacy. *Pay-per-view*.

THE COOPERS

On Monday, May 25, 2020, Memorial Day—the United States holiday commemorating the military service of its veterans who have died in combat—our nation remained gripped in a centuries-long race war evidenced by two "unrelated" events: one in Minneapolis, the other in Manhattan; the murder of George Floyd and the meeting of the Coopers.

Christian Cooper, a 57-year-old cisgender gay man, who lives on the Lower East Side, is an avid birder, and Black. Amy Cooper, a 40-year-old cisgender woman, who lives on the Upper West Side with her cocker spaniel, Henry, is white. Their racial identities feature prominently in their unintended meeting in the Ramble, as does White-sex Supremacy. "The two Memorial Day incidents captured on video two facets of entrenched racism Black people experience: one the horrors of police brutality, the other the routine humiliations and threats in daily life" (Maslin Nir, 2020, para. 5). Rarely, however, is white media explicit about the *sexualized* aspects of these routine humiliations and threats. The critical conceptualization of White-sex Supremacy aims to change that.

Racial Trauma and Time

Time, Menakem (2020) reminds us, functions in a manner that decontextualizes trauma:

> When we're talking about trauma, when we're talking about historical trauma, intergenerational trauma, persistent institutional trauma—and personal traumas, whether that be childhood, adolescence, or adulthood—those things, when they are left constricted, you begin to be shaped around the constriction. And it is wordless.
>
> (para. 13)

That the shapeshifting of Black bodies around trauma happens silently—
wordlessly—without Whitepeople having a clue, is the first thing we need to
reconcile as Whitepeople, given how logocentrism, as discussed in Chapter
2, discounts what we do not have words for. The strictures of language and
the forward thrust of white time bypass Black suffering caused by White-
supremacist trauma, erasing Black bodies and sexualities in the process. A
white-spun positive outlook is insufficient for healing the extent of trauma
incurred by Black bodies under White Supremacy. As poet Audre Lorde
(1984/2007) said: "The master's tools will never dismantle the master's
house" (pp. 110–113).

Trauma Bonding

The media is quick to clarify that Amy Cooper and Christian Cooper are not
related. I, on the other hand, argue they are. History and White-sex Supremacy
bind them (and their ancestors) in the present (and back through generations) as
sure as blood does, given trauma's propensity to bond (Dutton & Painter, 1993).
"Love too often perpetuates trauma, repeating the patterns of intimacy and pain
so many of us experienced growing up in racist and/or hetero-patriarchal environments" (brown, 2019, p. 62).

Typically applied to dynamics within abusive intimate relationships,
trauma bonding theory is relevant here. Trauma bonding establishes an emotional and psychological attachment to abusers for the abused based on repeti-
tive cycles of abuse within intimate partnerships (Dutton & Painter, 1993).
Given how mutuality and interdependency form the basis of intimate relationships, trauma bonding is a two-way street, developing codependency. However, while the dependency of Black people on Whitepeople is baked into the
racist system of White Supremacy, causing lack of freedom and choice for
Black people, the dependency Whitepeople have on Black people to maintain
their privileged status typically goes unrecognized by whites.

Devaluation and Positive Reinforcement

Trauma bonding sustains abusive relationships through devaluation and positive
reinforcement. Similarly, racism and sex positivity erect and maintain the "trauma
bond" inherent in White-sex Supremacy between Black bodies and white bodies. White-sex Supremacy is a system of sexual violence that uses sex-positive
discourses, historically and today, as a means to reinforce White Supremacy by
encouraging sexual assimilation and failing to critically examine race-evasive
rhetoric and the role rape and threat of rape play in discursive White-sex.

Whereas White Supremacy decenters and evades the intimate, racialized,
sexual aspects of trauma-bonding, White-sex Supremacy as a critical concept
recenters the racist and sexually violent nature of trauma bonding to move the
so-called private, intimate, and sexual aspects of racial trauma into the public

and political arena, as Black feminisms encourage us to do. This is so we can observe, study, and reconcile our racist and *rape-centric* Whiteculture.

Radical Play Act

- **Reflect on the heterosexist *color of rape:***

  - **If you identify as a white woman, have you ever been afraid of being raped by a Black man, for no valid reason except that he is Black?**
  - **If you identify as a white man, have you ever been concerned that a woman you know might be raped by a Black man, for no valid reason except that he is Black?**
  - **If you identify as a white genderqueer person, how do you relate to the aforementioned scenarios?**

Race-Based Emotions

"Emotions are not ancillary to the experience of racism, but are central to how racism affects individuals" (Grzanka et al., 2020, p. 48). Racism's emotional impact is not relegated to discreet personal experiences (as psychologists typically characterize them) but is fundamental to our collective sociocultural conditioning regarding race (Spanierman & Cabrera, 2015). Given that "shame might be the only thing more prevalent [than trauma], which leads to trauma being hidden, silenced, or relegated to a certain body of people" (brown, 2019, p. 62), race-based (sexual) shame needs to be addressed by Black people and Whitepeople alike. However, because "White shame . . . may obscure the consequences of White racial emotions for combatting racism and promoting social justice" (Grzanka et al., 2020, p. 49), I will focus on *white guilt.*

White Guilt

Whereas race-based sexual shame for Black people is connected with systemic inequities and internalized racism, raced-based sexual shame for Whitepeople aligns with white guilt, an individual and collective experience. White guilt produces mixed consequences—from motivating antiracist behavior to defensiveness, disconnection, and blame. Research on the *psychosocial costs of racism to Whites* (Spanierman et al., 2009, 2012; Todd et al., 2011; Spanierman & Heppner, 2004) demonstrates how emotion impacts our experience of racism as Whitepeople. Importantly, racism does not affect Whitepeople like Black people, who experience systemic disadvantages along with emotional, psychological, and physical trauma. While there are psychological consequences of racism for Whitepeople, such as race-based guilt, "reverse racism" is *not* one. Importantly, our relationship to white guilt can shift over time, resulting in increased awareness of our racial privilege (Garriott et al., 2015), especially regarding our sexuality, which is my aim here.

Sexual Positivity and Optimism

Stating the obvious: positivity is a privileged position, especially when it comes to race. It is easier to *choose happiness, look on the bright side*, or *see the glass half full*, when possessing socially conferred racial privilege. In other words, there is a lot more to be positive about when we are secure in our whiteness.

The senseless murder of George Floyd seemed to drive that point home for Whitepeople, who were unable to rationalize it away even with positive thinking (e.g., *everything happens for a reason*). However, the inhumanity of George Floyd's murder was not the result of barbaric cruelty by a solo actor (though there was that), or collusion by three additional actors, also Minneapolis police officers (though there was that too), but due to systems-wide failures, including policing that itself is a symptom of White Supremacy rather than a cause (Alexander, 2011; Russell-Brown, 2009).

At All Costs

Logocentric positivity is entrenched in individualistic culture. In America, success is purportedly achieved by *pulling yourself up by your bootstraps*, equating failure—to be happy, healthy, wealthy versus unhappy, sick, poor— as the near-exclusive fault of the individual, rather than the result of social, political, and structural factors. Those whose social identities place them on the margins have a harder time "going it alone" because the system does not support them. The idea that we do not—*should* not—need help fuels racial exceptionalism, obvious in my cousin's insistence that Obama got elected president as evidence of our post-racial state.

It would serve us to reclaim the original meaning of the idiom "pulling yourself up by your boot straps" for the purposes of developing *playmind* (detailed in Chapter 7), given that prior to the 1920s it meant *attempting to do something absurd* (Bologna, 2018). Like eradicating White-sex Supremacy.

Up by the Boot Straps

Pulling oneself up by one's bootstraps (referencing the finger hooks on the sides of boots circa nineteenth century) is physically impossible. No matter how hard you try, you cannot hoist yourself into the air. Currently, the idiom is used for blaming system inequities on individuals, particularly Black people, making it a well-disguised racist trope stressing individual effort and positivity over institutionalized racism.

Positive thinking blames BIPOC for failing to *achieve* whiteness, similar to how it blames cancer patients for getting cancer and failing to cure themselves (i.e., *didn't try hard enough, didn't think positively enough*) given the inference that positivity cures *dis*-ease (Ehrenreich, 2009). The real problem, however, is *discomfort* not negativity.

Surveillance of Negative Threats

Positivity acts as a *mechanism of surveillance* by scanning for *threats of negativity* due to the discomfort and *dis*-ease it causes the host. The tyranny of positive thinking forms the basis of sex positivity as it has entered the mainstream. Notably, "sex-positive" Google searches have increased substantially since 2008; new interest spurred by unexamined claims that sex positivity is "beneficial" (Ivanski & Kohut, 2017). Sex positivity is no longer strictly the basis for a transgressive political movement but appears in *Cosmo* as conventionally sound sex advice (Common Era, 2012; Nelson, 2021; Mosher, 2017; Ivanski & Kohut, 2017).

While there is no agreed-upon definition for sex positivity (Ivanski & Kohut, 2017), it is considered to be overwhelmingly *positive*. A contemporary antidote to sex negativity among "sex-positive" sexuality professionals, sex positivity (including its negative traces) has existed throughout history in *waves* (Mosher, 2017), predominantly *white* waves.

Waves of (White) Sex Positivity

Like white feminisms, waves of sex positivity fail to address the influence White Supremacy has on sex-negative *and* sex-positive culture. Sexology's early sexual reform movement promoted sex-positive discourses, flourishing until the Nazis raided Hirschfeld's Institute burning sex-affirming books in the street, closing sexological institutes and journals, and imprisoning sexologists (Irvine, 1990/2005). Early "positive" sexual reformers, such as Margaret Sanger and Henry Havelock Ellis, were also eugenicists, who advocated for untested birth control on Puerto Rican women; Planned Parenthood's services to be located in low-income communities of color; and forced sterilization of poor, Black and Brown, and/or mentally unstable women (Schuller, 2021; Mosher, 2017; Eig, 2014).

First Wave

Occurring during the late 1800s through the early 1900s, sex positivity's *first wave* includes the conception of *sexualwissenchaft* (German for *sexual science*, translated as *sexology*) by Iwan Bloch, an advocate for the scientific study of sexuality to reduce its moral stigma. The field of sexology grows rapidly, as institutes, journals, and sexological associations are established. By the early 1930s, approximately 80 sexual reform organizations with 350,000 members (including doctors, professionals, laypeople, etc.) offer medical and sexual counseling (Mosher, 2017). Magnus Hirschfeld, a German physician and sexologist, promotes homosexuality as both *universal* and *normal*. These contributions are critical counterarguments to sex-negating "self-proclaimed sexual experts" who "created taxonomies of 'perverts' and 'sexual deviants,' referring to homosexual, transsexual, sadist, masochist, fetishist, and exhibitionist individuals" (Mosher, 2017, p. 489).

Second Wave

In the *second wave*, during 1930s through the 1950s, Wilhelm Reich coins the term "sexual revolution" to underscore how (1) political revolution necessitates the overthrow of sexual oppression; (2) sexual expression is germane to human development; and (3) orgasms promote optimal health (Mosher, 2017). Female sexuality is newly centered in Simone de Beauvoir's (1949/2011) *The Second Sex*, reframing gender and sexuality as social constructs, questioning their patriarchal underpinnings (Mosher, 2017).

Third Wave

The *third wave*, during the 1960s through 2000s, establishes sex as a political act that is oppressive *and* liberatory, making negativity and positivity fundamental to sexuality. Political theorist and literary critic, Michel Foucault (1976/1990), himself a gay man, debunks the sex-negative "repressive hypothesis" by demonstrating how the proliferation of sex occurs *discursively*, with hegemonic power structures policing sex through technologies (e.g., sex education, sex therapy) and medicalization (e.g., psychiatry) to establish a sociocultural (white) heterosexist status quo that is race-evasive. The Hite Report (1976/2004), a study involving thousands of women, confirms that intercourse does *not* typically lead to female orgasm, whereas clitoral stimulation (found to be 70% more effective) does. The third wave also establishes lesbian sexuality (Rich, 1980), bisexuality (Queen, 1997/2002), queer sexuality (Butler, 1990/1999, 1993/2011; Halberstam, 2005, 2011; Muñoz, 1999, 2009), and sexual fluidity (Diamond, 2008), all of which challenged patriarchal and heteronormative assumptions about sexuality, and to some extent (though less so) its whiteness.

Noxious Positivity

For the purposes of this discussion, I prefer the word "noxious" over "toxic" as an adjective to describe the positivity prevalent in the sex-positive movement today. As we have seen in the aforementioned waves, the sex-positive movement has been a necessary counter to sex-negative culture, with traces of sex negativity in it. In "The Negative in Sex-positive," Kim Loliya (2019) defines negative as the "thoughts, feelings, and behaviors that disempower, cause harm or suffering, restrict choice or agency, and generally remove us from our more optimal states of being" (p. 31) often caused by sociocultural conditioning and policing.

While *toxic* and *noxious* have similar meanings, toxicity is thought to be more lethal. Sustained exposure to toxins, like White Supremacy, certainly kills, yet the *insidiousness* of White Supremacy might be its most pressing danger—like a noxious weed that spreads among people within democratic systems through generations, across space, place, and time.

Sexual Consent

Sex-positive discourses emphasize the importance of sexual consent. The problem is that Whitepeople fail to recognize that the intergenerational trauma Black bodies historically and currently endure centers on being *deprived of consent*. In a book on sex positivity, titled *Sex-positive: Redefining our Attitudes to Love and Sex*, Kelly Neff (2020) defines the sex-positive movement the way most sexuality professionals do—devoid of a racialized context—to appear innocuous, beneficial, and (most misleading) *anti*racist:

> The sex positive movement is a social, political and philosophical move-ment that promotes and embraces sexuality and sexual expression, with an emphasis on safe and consensual sex. Sex-positive relationships are ones where partners support each other's choices and decisions without judgement, guilt or slut shaming. In a sex positive relationship, you can be whoever you want sexually, and do whatever you want sexually, without having to apologize for your sexual identity or expression, so long as you are not causing real harm to anyone else.
>
> (Neff, 2020, p. 9)

My question is this: How does the idea of sexual consent impact body–minds that are deprived of consent (historically and presently) by White Supremacy? White settler sexuality educators, counselors, therapists, and researchers must be aware of and prepared to address this. I begin by (1) claiming my whiteness and white privilege; (2) acknowledging that White Supremacy is always-already in the room when we talk about sex; and (3) understanding that sex-positive values and rhetoric are based on historical and current race-evasive discourses, including civilization, normality, erotic love and marriage, sexual health and betterment, and sex positivity—the widely searched Google term that lacks definition consensus, inferring goodness alongside the erroneous implication that sexual consent is equally accessible to all when it is not.

Three-Fifths Consent

Historically, only rarely were Black bodies counted as people by Whitepeo-ple, and then only due to economic and/or political benefit to whites. The

Three-Fifths Compromise, for example, counted five slaves as three people, ensuring that Southern states controlled enough votes in the House of Representatives to keep from abolishing slavery. Today, similar movements are underway (e.g., voter redistricting, stricter voter registration) to disenfranchise people of color further, and undercount them. Historical racist accuracy (i.e., historicity) and practices allow us to conclude that a three-fifths person has three-fifths consent (perhaps less) when it comes to sexual choices, sexual safety, and sexual freedom.

White Talisman

If sex positivity was engineered to be an effective counterargument to sex -negativity (Libby, 2016), it performs fairly effectively. Yet the counternarrative also creates an unexamined positive spin with feel-good vibes that make sex positivity a talisman for *lusty white* sex, based on sexual liberation and enlightenment. Roger Libby, who coined the term "sex-positive" says this:

> Being sex-positive means affirming sexual open, joyous sexual freedom and consensual, *lusty* [emphasis added] pleasure. It means supporting rather than stifling sexually free and uplifting choices and offering sex education that is pro-sexual rather than antisexual (as with the current emphasis on abstinence).
>
> (Simply Sexy Editorial Team, 2014, para. 4)

Lusty fervor focused on *personal pleasure* remains ignorant of its Anglocentrism, even as it exists in a confused and racist sociopolitical climate where positive sexuality always-already contains traces of negativity. No matter how sexually optimistic we are, our sex-positive vibes fail to ensure only positiveness.

Liberation or Freedom?

"Enlightened" sex positivity among otherwise knowledgeable sexuality professionals infers sexual liberation that is psychic, behavioral, and even spiritual. And also guaranteed. However, despite its grand claims, sex positivity fails to deliver on its promises of sexual freedom, diluted by White-supremacist sociocultural restrictions on consent, pleasure, and well-being for marginalized bodies of color, and the "commodification of the liberatory impulse" (Nelson, 2021, p. 75), to peddle heteronormative (and its "kinky") white desire as fundamentally positive.

> Instead of the pressure to have penis-in-vagina sex and show how much you're enjoying it, now there's a pressure to do a range of sexual things

and show that you're enjoying them. In other words, there's still a sex hierarchy with one form of sex being seen as better than another. As soon as we have any kind of hierarchy—with one kind of sex as the ideal—some people are going to be excluded and stigmatized, and some people are going to feel pressured to have that kind of sex.

(Barker & Hancock, 2019, pp. 24–25)

Sex Critical

Many sexuality professionals critique and complexify sex positivity, including its kinky and queer elements, substituting the negative–positive binary with being *sex critical*, so that kinky sex and "vanilla" sex are equally examined and critiqued.

Being sex critical means that we can ask who is being included and excluded in any form of sex, event, or piece of writing. It also means being really aware of power dynamics that might cause people to feel pressured, or struggle to give informed consent.

(Barker & Hancock, 2019, p. 25)

Regarding its complexity:

Sex-positivity is the perspective that the only measure of a sexual act or practice is the consent, pleasure, and well-being of the people who do it—and the people who are affected by it. Any other judgements, attitudes, or feelings that one might have about it are likely to be reflections of one's own perspective rather than anything about that sexual act or practice. Having said that, each of these ingredients is *far more complex* [emphasis added] than they might first appear.

(Glickman, 2019, p. 20)

Included in its complexity is sex positivity's promise of sexual liberation. Issuing a cautionary warning in this regard, Maggie Nelson's treatise *On Freedom* distinguishes between *sexual liberation* and *sexual freedom*, relegating sexual liberation to homogenized and commodified (white) *sex that sells*, whereas sexual freedom is more heterogeneous and enduring. The sex (a.k.a. feminist or porn) wars of the 1970s forecast this liberatory shortcoming (and disillusionment) in sex positivity's third wave, explaining:

The end of the sex wars did not bring with it the more liberated world that feminists . . . envisioned. Instead, the nuanced pro-sex position . . . gave way to a more individualistic and conciliatory approach to women's rights—one that focused not on the second wave's project of 'liberation' but on a simpler, less ambitious, and more market-friendly idea of empowerment.

(Donegan, 2019, as cited in Nelson, 2021, p. 74)

Sex positivity has fared no better, with mass-produced sexuality being the result of the pro-sex movement: "What remains is a simulacrum of freedom: at one end, the ultimate symbols of marketable feminine sexuality protesting objectifications; at the other, legions of ordinary joes opening e-mails urging, 'Get bigger, last longer, become the beast she always wanted'" (Nelson, 2021, p. 75).

Although the focus of Nelson's treatise on (sexual) freedom does not interrogate White Supremacy directly, it complexifies power in a way that is useful for our work as White sexuality professionals: "Power relations are possible only insofar as the subjects are free. If one of them were completely at the other's disposal and became his thing, an object on which he could wreak boundless and limitless violence," as is the case for Black bodies under White Supremacy, "there wouldn't be any relations of power" (Foucault, 1997, as cited in Nelson, 2021, p. 79). The *lack of power relations* under White Supremacy causes perpetual asymmetry between Black and white people, diminishing the capacity for sexual freedom among Black bodies, making it imperative that we (re)envision sex positivity as occurring within a state of *freedom from*.

Freedom From Versus Freedom To

Critics of sex positivity—of which I am one—argue that *freedom to* (e.g., experience white sexual liberation at the expense and erasure of Black bodies and sexualities) has taken precedent over *freedom from* (e.g., sexual violence, sexual discrimination, and sexual coercion of Black bodies) creating dysconscious sex positivity that lacks racial scrutiny and antiracist revisioning, requiring a reexamination of what consent and sexual pleasure mean.

And Pleasure?

Next to consent, pleasure is the other most frequently cited feature of sex positivity (Glickman, 2019; Ivanski & Kohut, 2017). In "Looking Ahead: Justice and the Future of Sex-positivity," Dawn Serra asks: "How do we, as a community committed to pleasure and human connection, embrace the decolonization of our thought models and language when it comes to sex, gender, love, and relationship" (p. 214)? This query implies different approaches by Black people and Whitepeople. For example, *decolonizing pleasure* is critical for Black bodies (brown, 2019), whose bodies were colonized using the White-supremacist weaponry of sex, including rape and discursive White-sex, making pleasure confusing and illusive, whereas unsettling white bodies and *undoing imperialist assumptions* is critical to our antiracist work as white sexuality professionals.

While sexual consent and pleasure are key facets of sex positivity, pleasure need not be framed "positively" to feel good, given the complexity of feeling good—sexually and otherwise. Pleasure is not a simple proposition. Feeling good may—and in my experience often does—*feel bad* before it feels better, particularly as we as Whitepeople grapple with the implications of White-sex Supremacy on our own and others' sexualities.

Radical Honesty

In *Pleasure Activism*, adrienne maree brown (2019) reminds us that radical honesty is a self-taught behavior, necessary for addressing White-supremacist trauma: "We have to engage in an intentional practice of honesty to counter . . . socialization" (p. 61). We are socialized that love is a finite resource (brown, 2019) and sexuality devoid of race, causing Whitepeople to resist change that we do not feel responsible for. We are the inheritors—rather than originators—of White Supremacy, so our commitment to undoing imperialist White-sex is often tentative at best, because it is uncomfortable to change. Yet inheritance comes with responsibility, starting with telling the truth (about What Is).

Optimal Sexuality

Good–bad, positive–negative binaries are too simplistic for the complex terrain of sexuality. In fact, research into *optimal sex*—described as achieving a *qualitatively higher (sexual) plateau*—is *not* predicated on positivity, or even pleasure though it infers optimism (Kleinplatz & Ménard, 2007, 2020; Kleinplatz et al., 2009, 2020). Rather, optimal sexuality conceives of and promotes human erotic potential, including qualities of presence, authenticity, emotional connectivity, sexual and erotic intimacy, extraordinary communication, interpersonal risk-taking, vulnerability, and transcendence (Kleinplatz & Ménard, 2007, 2020; Kleinplatz et al., 2009, 2020; Wade, 2004), most of which would enhance our racial awareness as Whitepeople.

It should be noted that two key components of optimal sexuality—risk-taking and vulnerability—frequently evoke "negative" emotions, a descriptor I avoid when characterizing sexuality, given that emotions vary in intensity, cultural sensitivity, and uniqueness rather than goodness or badness, though they may be difficult to experience. Additionally, optimal sexuality does not rely on "normal" sexual functioning. Individuals who report having optimal sexual experiences do so despite "their own or their partners' diminishing genital responsiveness and overall physical ability with age, illness and disability" (Kleinplatz et al., 2009, p. 10).

The conflation of "good" with "normal" is a standard-bearer of noxious positivity (Kashdan & Biswas-Diener, 2014; Ehrenreich, 2009). Importantly, "negativity" when framed as sub-optimal even undesirable is not an impediment to experiencing optimal sexuality. I want to emphasize the *value of negativity* in the context of sexuality, particularly for Whitepeople, given that White Supremacy conflates "normal" and "good" with white privilege, forming the basis of discursive White-sex Supremacy, explained in more detail in Chapter 6. Importantly, optimal sexuality is a heightened state of attunement, awareness, and attention, which is why this book concludes with mindfulness-based practices for antiracist embodiment.

Arguably, sex positivity is valuable. It is formed in response to sex-negative culture that sexually shames, causing harm. Unfortunately, due to the rise of the (mostly white) "comfortable class" (Kashdan & Biswas-Diener, 2014) with ties to noxious positivity, emotional, mental, and social discomfort is regarded as unpleasant and unmanageable, thus avoided. A primary reason Whitepeople resist engaging in conversations about White Supremacy is due to *feel-good positivity bias* (Kashdan & Biswas-Diener, 2014).

Shame of Shame

There is a way in which sex positivity can *shame* sexual shame—blaming the victim, rather than sociocultural conditioning as perpetrator. Repeatedly, I have heard students and clients alike express shame about their sexual shame—as if they should be over their sexual trauma already—intensifying their suffering. Sex positivity has infiltrated the mainstream to the extent that most people have cursory knowledge of it, even when no formal definition exists (Ivanski & Kohut, 2017). In this way, sex positivity, like whiteness, polices psyches and bodies—via positively focused rhetoric—regarding how to think, feel, and behave sexually.

Sex negativity is reductionistic and problematic, reducing sex and sexuality to preset behaviors centering cisgender heterosexual sex focused on reproduction, aligning with eugenicist goals of White Supremacy. It labels marginalized sexual identities, desires, and behaviors as deviant, ostracizing transgender, fluid, queer, bisexual, pansexual, consensually non-monogamous, asexual, and so on, people (Mosher, 2017). On the other hand, sex positivity in principle, if not practice, focuses on expanding the definition of "normal," becoming more inclusive of "the range of fluid sexual experiences" (Mosher, 2017, p. 48; Queen, 1997/2002; Burnes et al., 2017; Gabosch & Shub, 2019; Neff, 2020). Still, critically unexamined sex positivity falls prey to White Supremacy, making sexuality an invention of White Supremacy and positivity the buoy that keeps it afloat.

5   The Making of White Sex

In *Making Sex: Body and Gender from the Greeks to Freud*, Thomas Laqueur (1990) writes: "Sometime in the eighteenth century, sex as we know it was invented" (p. 149). For accuracy, I would amend the quote to read: *Sometime in the eighteenth century [White]sex as we know it was invented. [It is what we call sex.]*

Laqueur (1990) is referring to how anatomical reproductive structures, once emblematic of a hierarchical universal order based on *one* sexual body, became *two* distinct and finite sexual bodies for earthly and gendered purposes, with onus on the female:

> The reproductive organs went from being paradigmatic sites for displaying hierarchy, resonant through the cosmos, to being the foundation of incommensurable difference: "women owe their manner of being to their organs of generation, and especially to the uterus," as one eighteenth-century physician put it.
>
> (p. 149)

One Sex

The social construction of gender remains tied to biological sex, once thought to be unary rather than binary. The Greek philosopher, physician, and surgeon, Aelius Galenus (anglicized as *Galen*), also known as the *father of anatomy*, said:

> Think first, please, of the man's [external genitalia] turned in and extending inward between the rectum and the bladder. If this should happen, the scrotum would necessarily take the place of the uterus with the testes lying outside, next to it on either side.
>
> (Laqueur, 1990, p. 25)

Because "you could not find a single male part left over that had not simply changed its position" (Laqueur, 1990, p. 26), Galen reasoned that anatomy

DOI: 10.4324/9781003190035-6

confirmed rather than two distinct sexes with separate reproductive organs, there is only *one*—decidedly *male*—sex. The subsequent, *inverted* and "faulty" version is referred to as *female*, the lesser sex and subservient gender, whose sociocultural role is reproduction. The lowly sex–gender is biblically (mis)understood to be created from Adam's rib to help carry out God's work of regeneration.

Homologous Structure

While homologous structure is a fact of reproductive anatomy—for example, the clitoris and penis, as well as the labia majora and minora and scrotum develop from the same tissue—Galen's conclusion that the "female" sex is an inverted, faulty, *lesser* version of the "male" is wholly inaccurate. In fact, homologous structure reveals more commonality than difference. However, we will learn in the next chapter that *anatomic binary "distinctiveness"* erases homologous facticity to create corporeal theatrics that establish and maintain White-sex Supremacy relying on biological sexual difference. The homologous facticity of reproductive structures always comes as a surprise to my students when I teach about it, serving as a pertinent example of how the human sciences (e.g., biology, psychology) strengthen and maintain sociocultural sexual narratives, using the sexed and gendered body to establish, legitimize, and maintain racist and sexist hierarchies.

The one-sex/one-flesh model, like the two-sex/two-flesh model that usurps it, creates a racist and misogynistic bodily hierarchy, rendering a *white* woman's body a flawed version, or poor facsimile, of a *white* man's: "Instead of being divided by their reproductive anatomies, the sexes are linked by a common one. [White] women, in other words, are inverted, and hence less perfect, [white] men" (Laqueur, 1990, p. 26). Nevertheless, the flawed female body ranks categorically superior to the Black (male and/or female) body. Racial hierarchy develops white feminist thought, distorting liberal ideals of citizenship, democracy, and the body (Schuller, 2021; Newman, 1999; Caldwell & Leighton, 2018), such that the fixity of the white body renders it a reliable site for the cultural reproduction of whiteness, through asexual (i.e., discursive) and heterosexist (i.e., sex = intercourse) methods.

From One Sex to Two Sexes

Ultimately, one flesh becomes two discreet bodies—biological sexes and social genders—through the process of reproductive differentiation, such that sex (distinctly *heterosexual* sex) becomes "scientifically" established as occurring between two anatomically *heterogenous bodies:* one male, one female, who in a parallel process became *homogenously white*—referring to those who are deemed taxonomically "superior" (i.e., "cultured" Europeans) (Laqueur, 1990; Irvine, 1990/2005; Kendi, 2016). The heterogeneity of biological sex and the homogeneity of whiteness form the basis of what we call *sex*, understood to be synonymous with *White-sex* or *racist sex*, given its White-supremacist agenda, valuing discipline, fitness, reproduction, "health," and the degradation and subsequent erasure of Black (sexual) bodies.

There is rationale that women—the *female sex*—bear the weight of this new bodily hierarchy:

> As the natural body itself became the gold standard for social discourse, the bodies of women—the perennial other—thus became the battleground for redefining the ancient, intimate, fundamental social relation: that of man to man. Women's bodies in their corporeal scientifically accessible concreteness, in the very nature of their bones, nerves, and most important, reproductive organs, came to bear an enormous new weight of meaning. Two sexes, in other words, were invented as a new foundation for gender.
>
> (Laqueur, 1990, p. 150)

However, "women" bearing the weight of this recategorization is a mischaracterization. *Black* women bear the weight—then and now—given how their bodies (and humanness) are erased from the equation entirely, as their sex and gender intersect with race (Crenshaw, 1989). While (white) women are classified as lesser of the two sexes, it does not excuse them from being responsible for their racial privilege, eclipsing the (subhuman) status of Black women that is the consequential failure of white feminisms (Schuller, 2021; Newman, 1999).

Bodily Fixity and Consciousness

Relying on medical and philosophical literature from classical (i.e., white) antiquity to the end of the seventeenth century, Laqueur (1990) presents how the *one-sex/one-flesh* model dominates understanding of sexual difference during this time, arguing that while *gendered selves* occupy a more nuanced history that shifts as changes to society, culture, and religion occur, the *anatomical*—or bodily—*self* remains fixed.

White Disembodiment

Importantly, the fixed unary body referred to here is *always-already white*, shaped by imperial, colonial, and White-supremacist forces. However, the white body becomes *dis*embodied, forfeiting (white) embodiment in favor of (white) consciousness, which Locke philosophized as ranking superior to the (white) body: "Once man's hierarchy over the beast (via his body) is established, it is consciousness that is valorized" (Mohanram, 1999, p. 35). Locke's empiricism, and its influence on how we think and relate to ourselves and our world, has significant influence on scientific (and ultimately sexual) epistemologies, important to our work as white sexuality professionals.

From Bodily to Discursive Identity

While white and Black—*human* versus *bestial*—bodies are hierarchically constituted, such that the whiteness ranks superior to Blackness, there is dramatic shift away from (white) *bodily identity* toward *discursive identity* with the valorization of consciousness, whereby whiteness loses its corporeality (in favor of discursiveness) (Hare-Mustin, 1994; Iantaffi, 2012) and Blackness retains it: "Yes, we are—we Negroes—backward, simple, free in our behavior. That is because for us the body is not something opposed to what you call the mind. We are in the world" (Fanon, 1967/1986, pp. 126–127).

The forfeiture of bodily identity for discursive identity forms the basis of White-sex supremacy and its performative disembodiment. Despite its valorization, white performativity hinges on *dysconsciousness*—or lack of critical examination—whereas Blackness, according to Fanon (1967/1986), is consciously (albeit also secretly) performed:

> The white man transcends and transforms the body into will and rationale, a perception, and a perspective, whereas the black man embodies the Body. Though the Negro functions as other to the White, however, it is within this location of otherness that a trace of alterity can be found: "The white man had the anguished feeling that I was escaping from him and that I was taking something with me. . . [I]t was obvious that I had a secret."
> (Fanon, 1967/1986, p. 128; Mohanram, 1999, p. 27)

Sexualized corporeal theatrics, as we will learn in Chapter 6, is a conjoint performance of white dysconsciousness and Black consciousness, where white disembodiment meets Black embodiment in splacetime.

Radical Play Act

- **Consider your relationship with your body. Now consider your relationship with your *white* body.**
  - **How are they different/similar?**
- **Consider your relationship with your consciousness. Now consider your relationship with your *white* consciousness.**
  - **How are they different/similar?**
- **How are you embodied? How are you disembodied?**
- **What is the cost of your disembodiment to Black bodies?**

From One (Human) Race to Racial Hierarchy

The anatomical recategorization that establishes the two-sex model reconceives hierarchy from within a single bodily category to between bodily categories, thus pitting sexual bodies against each other: *male versus female.*

> Organs that had shared a name—ovaries and testicles—were now linguis-
> tically distinguished. Organs that had not been distinguished by a name of
> their own—the vagina, for example—were given one. Structures that had
> been thought common to man and woman—the skeleton and the nervous
> system—were differentiated so as to correspond to the cultural male and female.
>
> (Laqueur, 1990, pp. 149–150)

The discursive shift from establishing hierarchy *within* a category to *between* categories based on reproductive anatomy allows for a similar and concurrent hierarchical reconfiguration of the cultural body based on the invented
category of race, creating new sociocultural sites (e.g., male, female, white,
Black) for interpreting sexuality based on *scientific* (purportedly biological
and "natural") *fact* that itself is a misnomer. The accurate term is *scientific
racism* (Irvine, 1990/2005; Kendi, 2016; Saini, 2019) which accentuates
difference in kind over difference in degree.

Scientific Racism

Instead of one race (i.e., the human race), racial categories were "scientifically" established, supporting racial hierarchy, and cementing the trauma of
White Supremacy *in the body* (i.e., White-body Supremacy). New "scientific
evidence" ranked bodies according to geography, aesthetics, and difference
in kind. For example, the Caucasoid race was determined to be superior to
Negroid and Mongoloid races (Painter, 2010). This, despite the fact that
the (racist) science of racialized bodies is fiction. Here, we observe how
biology—considered "irrefutable" bodily science—is used to validate a pur-
ported *higher truth*, meaning one that aligns with hegemonic cultural narratives and power structures.

> Anatomy, and nature as we know it more generally, is obviously not pure
> fact, unadulterated by thought or convention, but rather a richly compli-
> cated construction based not only on observation, and on a variety of social
> and cultural constrains on the practice of science, but on *aesthetics of rep-
> resentation* [emphasis added] as well. Far from being the foundations for
> gender, the male and female bodies in eighteenth- and nineteenth-century
> anatomy books are themselves artifacts whose production is part of the
> history of their epoch.
>
> (Laqueur, 1990, pp. 163–164)

Aesthetics of Representation

The aesthetics of representation—that emphasizes difference—becomes the basis upon which we talk about and perform White-sex Supremacy, which itself is an artifact of the (white) European and American bourgeoise (Foucault, 1976/1990). Ethnicity and classism, separately and combined, intersect with race to establish scientific racism that assigns lower status to ethnic and poor minorities, but who today in America assimilate as white, like the ethnic communities I grew up in (e.g., Polish, Italian, Irish, and German).

While early European anatomical science links reproductive anatomies to one decidedly male body, anatomical science in the late seventeenth and eighteenth centuries and its new epistemologies form distinct and opposing biological, sexual, and gendered categories further distinguished by race, facilitating the emergence of discreet and subversively linked terms and social conventions: *heterosexuality* and *whiteness* (Katz, 1995; Carter, 2007).

> While we see anger and violence in the streets of our country, the real battlefield is inside our bodies. If we are to survive as a country, it is inside our bodies where this conflict will need to be resolved.
> (Menakem, 2017, p. xvii)

I do not dispute Menakem's wisdom here. The work is at the site of the body. Black feminists have known this and advocated for it through the ages. I would add, that it must also be addressed *between* bodies—particularly Black and white bodies—where the real violence of White-sex Supremacy occurs, although white bodies have the privilege of not participating.

Between Bodies

In *Fearing the Black-body: The Racial Origins of Fat Phobia*, Strings (2019) shows how race acts as a *double agent*, impacting both Black and white bodies, by making Blackness savage and whiteness disciplined, particularly with regard to the assigned-female body. The sexual aesthetics of discipline and savagery—how to look and not look sexually; how to be and not be sexually; what to do and not do sexually—form the basis of modern racist White-sex through seemingly benign race-evasive language that emphasizes *normal*, which upon further investigation reveals White-supremacist underpinnings and the erasure of Black bodies (Carter, 2007).

Through aesthetic representation, athletic and disciplined whiteness becomes the foundation upon which normal modern (white) sex is taught, learned, and enacted. Not sexy sex, but *healthy* married heterosexual reproductive sex, given its eugenically based procreative purpose: to ensure continuity of fit *native whiteness* and its supremacy (Carter, 2007). Despite anthropological, archaeological, biological, and genetic evidence refuting the existence of pure and/or distinct races, ongoing concern among whites that whiteness may lose superiority—in numbers and power—miscegenation, immigration, and growing birth rates in non-European regions continue to be discouraged today (Saini, 2019). Indeed, "mainstream scientists, geneticists and medical researchers still invoke race and use these categories in their work, even though we have been told for 70 years that they have no biological meaning, that they have only social meaning" (Saini as cited in Skibba, 2019, para. 5).

Bodily Science: Sex and Race

The *science of sex* and the *science of race* arose in the same historical moment during the eighteenth century as new epistemologies gained scientific legitimacy by incorporating the taxonomic method of the natural sciences that Linnaeus and other European taxonomic "experts" used.

Human Taxonomies

François Bernier, a French intellectual and physician, created the first human taxonomy focused on race in the Western Hemisphere. Based on his travels, Bernier developed four idiosyncratic racial classifications centering geography, with *pride of place* belonging to Europe: (1) Europe, North Africa, the Middle East, India, Southeast Asia, and the Americas; (2) sub-Saharan Africa; (3) east/northeast Asia; and (4) the Sámi people (Painter, 2010). While Bernier may be known as the first taxonomist to contribute to the genesis of scientific racism, he certainly was not the last. In 1735, the "father of modern taxonomy," Carl Linnaeus, a Swedish botanist, zoologist, and physician continued the practice of racial categorization, formalizing binomial nomenclature and hierarchy by creating subcategories of *Homo sapiens* based on race, focusing less on geographical terrain and more on the aesthetics of "character" and pubis:

> At the pinnacle of this human kingdom reigned H. s*apiens europaeus:* "Very smart, inventive. Covered by tight clothing. Ruled by law." Then came H. sapiens americannus ("Ruled by custom") and H. sapiens asiaticus ("Ruled by opinion"). He relegated humanity's nadir, H. sapiens afer to the bottom, calling this group "sluggish, lazy. . . [c]rafty, slow, careless. Covered by grease. Ruled by caprice," describing, in particular, the "females with genital flap and elongated breasts."
>
> (Kendi, 2016, p. 82)

Focusing squarely on the body, racist science deepens the (re)categorization of the reproductive body under the two-sex model. An example is Freud's *penis envy*, which hinges on the belief that the female body is constructed completely differently. Penial envy may have been less believable had there been acknowledgment that the clitoris and penis are homologous structures (i.e., derived from the same tissue) according to the one-sex model, despite its problems. With its 8,000 nerve endings on the tip alone (twice the amount of the penis), the clitoris has plenty of capacity for pleasure (Nagoski, 2015), perhaps even more so than the penis, making the up-power *gender status* of the male (more than his penis) the focus Freudian "penis" envy.

The anatomical reconceptualization of two sexes failed to reference homologous reproductive structures indicative of the one-sex model, where difference was predicated on degree rather than kind:

> Where at least two genders correspond to but one sex, where the boundaries between male and female are of degree and not of kind, and where the reproductive organs are but one sign among many of the body's place in a cosmic and cultural order that transcends biology.
>
> (Laqueur, 1990, p. 25)

Difference in Kind

Contrarily, the difference in kind rather than degree is critical to shaping whiteness and locating White Supremacy within the body, as it linguistically paves the way for the emergence of different races, beginning with the fallacy of polygenesis, and different origination stories. "That Negroes have stronger, coarser nerves than Europeans because they have smaller brains, and that these facts explain the inferiority of their culture, are parallel to those which held that the uterus naturally disposes women toward domesticity" (Laqueur, p. 155).

The links between bodily aesthetics (e.g., beauty), sexuality, gender, and race are well established (Strings, 2019; Gentles-Peart, 2018; Rottenberg, 2003; Morgan, 1997; Gilman, 1985). What is less understood, however, particularly among Whitepeople, including sexuality professionals, is the embeddedness of whiteness and White Supremacy in liberal *positively* focused sex. In fact, entire books (as their covers suggest) dedicated to "everything you need to know about sex-positivity" (i.e., *Sex-positive Now*) and "redefining our attitudes to love and sex" (i.e., *Sex-positive*) make no mention of the role White Supremacy plays in defining sex and sex positivity. While *sexual diversity* is a primary focus of the sex-positive movement and racial diversity and inclusion expressed values, critical examination of how White-supremacist rhetoric has influenced sex positivity is glaringly absent.

While sociocultural shifts (e.g., civil rights legislation, JEDI initiatives) and sex-positive rhetoric suggest racial progress, the racialized sexual body remains fixed under White-sex Supremacy. The fictionalized discursive difference between male and female and white and Black bodies as a matter of kind rather than degree makes sexuality a cultural site for White Supremacy, with a narrative that mischaracterizes sexuality as personal rather than social.

Personal Not Social, Disordered Not Diseased

As discussed, the science of sex and the science of race, having originated during the same historical period, use biology and taxonomic practices (like the natural sciences do) to establish scientific legitimacy, positing an essentialist (White-supremacist) person-centric perspective rather than socially constructed or interactionist ones; the latter focused on ongoing interaction between biological and social processes.

Science of Sex

The *science of sex* and its medicalization (Foucault, 1963/1994; Foucault, 1976/1990) further recharacterizes sex and sexual behavior as sexual disease, such that *sexual deviance* is reclassified as *sexual disorder* (e.g., from "pervert" to "invert") (Freud, 1905/1920), considered to be a "sex-positive" development with promise of treatment, even "cure." Whereas disease is a process of affliction with causes and symptoms, disorder is a disturbance to otherwise "normal" functions (Greenberg, 2014). The inference of "abnormal" is the hallmark of disorder creating normative hierarchies in sex. Its essentialist ascription (i.e., sex is natural) casts sex as a psychobiological rather than sociocultural phenomena with behavioral implications, effectively making sex *personal rather than social* when sex is always-already social, historically and today.

Science of Race

The *science of race* similarly relies on psychobiology to pathologize bodily pigment and facial features via pseudoscience (e.g., phrenology and physiognomy) as deviating from the norm of whiteness to become "abnormal." Thereby constructing a racialized and sexualized hierarchy under White Supremacy that translates to a Darwinian *survival of the Whitest*, buoying eugenicist ideology and racist medical practices performed on non-consenting Black bodies, such as sterilization and unnecessary experimentation in gynecological surgery, resulting in racialized sexual trauma that continues to impact and shape the field of human sexualities today (Irvine, 1990/2005; Laqueur, 1990).

Viewed from an essentialist perspective, sex becomes a psychobiological ruse that misses (and denies) the effects of White Supremacy on sexuality.

Undeniably, what we conventionally describe as sexual behavior is rooted in biological capacities and processes, but no more than other forms of behavior. . . . The sexual area may be precisely that realm wherein the superordinate position of the sociocultural over the biological level is most complete.

(Gagnon & Simon, 1973, p. 15)

The invention of "natural" racial and sexual hierarchies cements scientific racism: "The entire ladder and all of its steps—from Greeks or Brits at the very top down to the Angolans and Hottentots at the bottom—everything bespoke of ethnic racism" (Kendi, 2016, p. 83). While Africans who considered themselves hierarchically "superior" to other Africans supported ethnocentric ascension, they "rejected the racist ladder that deemed them inferior to White people" (Kendi, 2016, p. 83).

Threat of Rape

Building on essentialist (i.e., "natural")-based scientific discourse, discursive White-sex Supremacy guarantees *threat of rape*. The Black male rapist trope—comprised of "beastly Black men" desiring to rape white women—becomes pseudoscientific fodder. The Black rapists' white male counterparts are duty-bound to protect the sexual and racial purity of white women. After all, it is white women's work to *birth the Aryan nation*.

Under White-sex Supremacy, Black women are subject to *actual* rape and threat of rape (rather than discursive rape) by white men, making threat of rape racist weaponry of White-sex Supremacy. Yet it is *unfounded* fear of rape that weaponizes sex against Black men, giving *White heterosexual women* a powerful racist weapon at their disposal: fear of rape.

Following a class session that I was teaching on the topic, a white cisgender female student came up to me privately to ask: *But what if I'm legitimately afraid (with vocal emphasis on legitimately) of Black men?* Further explaining that she had been the bullied (never touched) by a group of Black boys in grade school, and felt frightened when she was around Black men. While I sympathized that her fear was real (feelings are), I encouraged her to consider that her fear likely intersects with the Black male rapist trope, which was something she had never considered. Hers is a ripe example of how the trauma of White Supremacy and its weaponization of sex become lodged in white bodies as White-sex Supremacy, making the sexualized component of White-body Supremacy explicit in White-sex Supremacy, which is critical for us as white sexuality professionals to identify and become individually and collectively responsible for.

Rape, Not Sex

As previously discussed, distinguishing rape from sex works similarly. By framing rape as "negative" and sex as "positive" Whitepeople distance ourselves from the sexual atrocities of White Supremacy. As a result, the discourses we employ to talk about sex become erroneously devoid of race, as if there is no trace of White Supremacy in sex positivity. As we will see more thoroughly in Chapter 6, *talk of "positive" sex* becomes cunningly race-evasive (Carter, 2007).

Radical Play Act

- **Do you distinguish *rape* from *sex?* *If so, how?***
  - **What are the benefits?**
  - **What are the drawbacks?**
  - **What are the racist implications?**

Because discursive sex positivity distinguishes rape from sex, it ignores and decenters the sexually violent impact of White Supremacy. As a critical concept, White-sex Supremacy serves to bring the racist and sexually violent nature of sex positivity, as a trauma-bonding mechanism, into our awareness in order to examine the sexualized aspects of racial trauma in the public performative arena, which I refer to here as *White-sex Theater.*

6 White-Sex Theater

Corporal Theatrics in Splacetime

According to Thinley Norbu (1998), author of *The Magic Dance*, sentient beings exist in time and space. This means that we *perceive*—seeing, hearing, touching, tasting, smelling, and thinking—within a particular space, place, and time (i.e., splacetime). That we are *conscious beings* and also *raced subjects* under White Supremacy forms the basis of our enlanguaged and embodied existence, causing racialized and sexualized reactivity (i.e., performativity) in splacetime, which I refer to as *White-sex Theater*. White-sex Theater relies on heterosexual whiteness, sex-positive discourse, and corporeal theatrics for its centuries-long run.

Heterosexual Whiteness

As a *sexual* organizing principle, heterosexual whiteness manifests discursively and performatively in a variety of ways, historically and currently, keeping White-sex Supremacy intact. This includes the differential diagnosis of *sexual neurasthenia* among sexually nervous whites, self-proclaimed heirs to modern civilization in the Gilded Age (Beard, 1880, 1881, 1884) establishing the basis for *white fragility; Norma and Normman*, life-size plaster replicas of (white) sexual "normality" on display at the Cleveland Museum of Health in the 1940s (Carter, 2007; Creadick, 2010; Stephens, 2015, 2018) representative of racial "progress" and used for sex education; *assimilative beauty practices* like blondness and thinness (Rankine, 2019; Strings, 2019); and *respectability politics* (Higginbotham, 1993; Starkey, 2015, 2016) whereby marginalized identities appease dominant standards of morality. More recently, heterosexual whiteness manifests as Karen memes, depicting performative reenactments of white fragility by entitled middle-aged white women (e.g., feigning fear of rape by Black men, like Amy Cooper) popularized on social media. These white performativities demonstrate that seemingly "positive" and/or race-evasive discourses of sexuality are complicit in the erasure of Black bodies.

DOI: 10.4324/9781003190035-7

Structural, Not Natural

Sex, like race, "is a structure not an event" (DiAngelo, 2018, p. 28). Neither sex nor race is an "indubitable feature of the natural world" (Coates, 2015, p. 7). Yet talk of sex, like talk of race, ascribes natural features and origins to socially constructed sexual fiction, rendering sex along with race "the innocent daughter of Mother Nature" (Coates, 2015, p. 7). The guise is effective, given how Whitepeople "deplore the Middle Passage or Train of Tears the way one deplores an earthquake, a tornado, or any other phenomenon that can be cast as beyond the handiwork of men" (Coates, 2015, p. 7). As a result, rape and threat of rape—the sexual legacy of White-sex Supremacy—is ignored in essentialist sexual discourses such as sexual consent that lacks critical examination of *who* is attempting to consent to sex and *with whom*.

Whitepeople distance ourselves from the White-supremacist origins of sex. When the sexual violence baked into Whiteculture is considered to be *something other than sex* (i.e., rape), we minimize our culpability. By framing *rape* as "negative" and *sex* as "positive," we further distance ourselves from the sexual atrocities of White Supremacy. As a result, the discourses we employ to discuss and understand sex become race-evasive, fomenting White-sex Supremacy's stronghold. Emphasizing "positiveness" also obscures our hidden commitment to race-evasive sexual discourse (Carter, 2007).

Sex-Positive Discourse

Enlanguaged and embodied corporeal theatrics are based on White-supremacist sex-positive discourses that include (past and present) psychiatric diagnoses, such as neurasthenia, hysteria, homosexuality, gender identity disorder, and gender dysphoria, that emphasize psychobiological rather than sociocultural causes. Discursive sex—including sex positivity—has a racially violent history that we cannot ignore. As white sexuality educators, counselors, and therapists, we must surface and address our complicity with heterosexual (and homosexual) whiteness to be effective antiracists in our field.

As defined in Chapter 2, sexual discourse is the dynamic social practice that constructs the parameters of our social world, including casual and professional mentions of sex. The casualness with which white sexuality professionals adopt a sex-positive ethos with no universal definition (Ivanski & Kohut, 2017) is based more on dysconsciousness than ethical discernment, given that most white professionals want to be perceived favorably—meaning *for* sex positivity and *against* sex negativity without critical examination of the role "positiveness" plays in Black-body erasure. White sexuality professionals must learn to interrogate who is included and who is left out of "positive" sexual discourses (Barker & Hancock, 2019) to understand how whiteness is running the show.

Naming Whiteness

According to Carter (2007), there are several reasons to examine the discursive normality of heterosexual whiteness; foremost, to force whiteness to name itself. White-sex and its self-congratulatory "naturalness" and "innocence" facilitates race-evasive sexual discourse that decouples Black bodies from what is sexually "normal" (i.e., white). Rather than employing historical racist rhetoric (e.g., Blackness is beastly), its tactic is assimilative, centering sexual health and wellness, such that Black sexual bodies are urged (and enticed) to "perform whiteness" by adopting markers of white sexual attractiveness, such as discipline, thinness, and blondness (Carter, 2007; Strings, 2019; Rankine, 2019).

Distinct, interrelated, and successive sexual discourses form a discursive "sex-positive" *menagerie* that lulls us into believing sex positivity is antiracist. I use "menagerie" deliberately, to underscore how white heterosexuality *domesticates* sex, placing it in captivity, so that its threatening qualities (e.g., chaos, wildness, Blackness) become *civilized*, like Eros. This is true of the following "sex-positive" discourses: *civilization discourse, normality discourse, erotic love and marriage discourse*, and *sexual health and betterment discourse*.

Civilization Discourse (1800s–1850s)

Civilization discourse advocates for sexual self-discipline and self-control (e.g., the "civilized" barbarian). It is patriarchal and sexist, admonishing sex before marriage for (white) women. It values "chastity" and "purity," making purity synonymous with whiteness, and white men its staunchest protectors. It is associated with nervousness and fragility. Modern whites are increasingly diagnosed with *neurasthenia* (Beard, 1880, 1881), as white upper-class men and women become *sexually exhausted* (Beard, 1884) by their "overwhelming responsibility" as "inheritors of modern civilization" tasked with the *literal* reproduction whiteness (Carter, 2007).

Normality Discourse (1860s–1940s)

Normality discourse subsumes civilization discourse, remaining White-supremacist but becoming race-evasive, with race rarely being mentioned and whiteness perceived as normal. Carefully disciplined reproductivity becomes paramount. Discourse shifts to normality, focusing on sexual health, white heterosexual marriage, and having babies.

NORMA AND NORMMAN

Changes in the body become inseparable from changes in civilization. The terra-cotta statues, **Norm**a and **Norm**man, come to personify White civilization's achievement in *aesthetic improvement*. Displayed at the 1930 World's Fair, and the wider public in the summer of 1945 at the Cleveland Health Museum, Norma and Normman represent the pride of (white) sexual "progress" and "normality" as statistical representations of the *Average American Boy and Girl*.

They are the reproductive heirs of modern (white) Americans, used to teach sex education and "sexual health" (Carter, 2007; Creadick, 2010; Stephens, 2015, 2018). The normality they represent is inseparable from their race (i.e., whiteness), even as their normality is formed and expressed through race-evasive codes and discourse. Normal (a.k.a. *white*) sex in America goes public, with Norma and Normman becoming icons of a constitutively white heterosexual eroticism in marriage.

Erotic Love and Marriage Discourse (1950s–Present)

Modern white heterosexuality becomes synonymous with a *way of life* (i.e., heteronormativity) not just sexual attraction. It runs concurrent with white flight, as Whitepeople move to the suburbs in droves during the Civil Rights (e.g., Black Power, Free Love) era. It symbolizes the "American" (a.k.a. white) values of marriage, family, procreation, legacy, and a 9–5 capitalistic work life. An erotic, sexually fulfilling marriage becomes a cultural necessity to keep white heterosexual couples together, as threat of "extinction" looms when white women begin working outside the home. Sexual pleasure for white men *and* women is newly advocated for in marital and sexual advice literature and newspaper columns (e.g., Dear Abby). Examples of newspaper headlines include "Norma's Husband Better Be Good!" and "Evolution Outlook Bright if Model Girl Weds Wisely" in the *Cleveland Plain Dealer*. This phase also ushers in the adoption of heteronormative ideals by white LGBT culture in what becomes known as *homonormativity* (Duggan, 2002).

Sexual Health and Betterment Discourse (1980s–Present)

Symbolized by a blue pill (i.e., Viagra) promising sexual enhancement and male virility, sexual health and betterment is characterized by the medicalization of sexuality and the incessant monitoring of (sexual and relational) "health" on a daily, even moment-by-moment, basis. Sexual self-help becomes a key feature of *do-it-yourself* sex positivity. And rather than disappearing, eugenicist ideology and practice are disguised in positive-seeming therapeutic agendas of *sexual betterment* operating within a doctrine of (sexual) *healthism* (Crawford, 1980; Carter, 2007, Barker, 2014).

Each of the aforementioned discourses employs sex positivity as a covert mechanism to support White-sex Supremacy.

Sex Positivity Then and Now

With no agreed-upon definition then or now, historical and current proponents of sex positivity cite a wide range of benefits, including sex education, marriage satisfaction, and the prevention of unwanted pregnancy and childhood sexual abuse (Ivanski & Kohut). Proponents of sex positivity also presume that sex-negative culture is more racist than sex-positive culture, given its puritanical (white) Christian roots, which is misguided.

Because "liberal" sex historically and presently centers around what Lomax (2018) aptly refers to as the *nuclear political project* (p. 203), meaning the exclusionary neoliberal doctrine of heteronormative and homonormative (Duggan, 2002) marriage and family (Marzullo, 2011), sexual consent and pleasure are not racist-free zones. Freud, for example, whose contributions incorporated pleasure into sex, making him a sex-positive proponent in his day, still considered *mature* sex—as opposed to *immature* (i.e., "inverted" or homosexual) sex—to be married, missionary, procreative, penis-in-vagina sex, whereby (white) husbands rather than their (white) wives are the focal point of sexual pleasure (Freud, 1905/1920).

Arguably, mature, consensual, pleasurable, marital sex focused on procreation is an early and ongoing example of sex positivity. While extending consensual, pleasurable, marital sex to include same-sex couples took time, it ultimately expanded neoliberalism's reach into intimate queer spaces, becoming a political device for feigning inclusion. In "Through a Glass, Darkly: U.S. Marriage Discourse and Neoliberalism," Marzullo (2011) suggests that shifting semantics make heterosexual and same-sex marriage a discursive mechanism for sociopolitical control, making the *body*—given its ability to communicate without language—a cultural site steeped in corporeal theatrics that is ripe for examination.

Corporeal Theatrics

I came across the term *corporeal theatrics* in *Making Sex: Body and Gender from the Greeks to Freud*, referenced in the previous chapter, by Laqueur (1990). It is used only once, at the start of Chapter 2, to encapsulate more than explain how "destiny" is determined by scientific narratives focused on the body. Laqueur (1990) uses the term to emphasize how differentiating reproductive anatomy—from one sex (i.e., male) to two sexes (i.e., male and female)—causes the body to become a cultural site based on the aesthetics of representation, a concept introduced in the last chapter to ameliorate the one-sex body by accentuating and weaponizing difference in kind via sexual hierarchy (e.g., male over female, heterosexual over homosexual) whereby power is socioculturally policed (Foucault, 1976/1990). Corporeal theatrics are based on dichotomous representations and enactments of the *sexed* and *gendered* body. To which I add *raced*.

I employ the term corporeal theatrics to underscore how the aesthetics of representation and difference are utilized under White-sex Supremacy. Specifically, how (re)enactments of whiteness encountering Blackness create a racist and sexualized theatrical performance under White Supremacy, which white sexuality professionals must make conscious—first, to ourselves.

Performing Whiteness in Sex

Like gender and sex, race is performed (Ehlers, 2012; Rottenberg, 2003). While performativity is not easily defined, it involves "the anticipation of an authoritative disclosure of meaning" (Butler, 1990/1999, p. xv) such that bodily identity (e.g., gender, sexuality, race) is derived externally by an "authorized" decider with *vested interest*—meaning the power and control *to decide*.

To better grasp the *sexual performativity* of White Supremacy, I expand Judith Butler's (2016) concept of gender performativity to include race in the following paragraph:

> One finds oneself inside a category not of one's own making. Of course, it is this particular body who suffers and enjoys, and no other, but that suffering and enjoyment is already a relational matter—gender [and race] is performed for a someone, even if that someone does not yet exist; and sexuality is lived in relation to a world of others, whether it is reclusive, auto-erotic, externalized, or exposed. When someone suffers as a consequence of having broken with a cultural norm, or for having shown how the norm can or must be broken or bent, that person has entered into a cultural and political struggle whether or not one meant to, whether or not there are proximate signs of others in solidarity. An isolated act can, in fact, be a radical petition for solidarity, as if to say, "Where are those of you who will support me now?" Gender is not gender [and race is not race] if it does not imply the social dimension of a bodily being, the way that the body refers to a broader world and exceeds the one who bears or does it, even as that one remains in some sense singular.
>
> (para. 6)

Made White

In the social construction of gender and race, race coopts gender whereby gender subsumes race. Gender is binarized (i.e., man-woman) and racialized—made *white*. Performing gender, meaning (white) *maleness*, (white) *femaleness*, (white) *masculinity*, and (white) *femininity* functions to establish and maintain White-sex Supremacy by making (white) *men* sexually virile and (white) *women* sexually fragile.

Because "non-whites" (Black people especially) are considered barbaric and thus *subhuman*, prototypical *white* sexuality becomes the *assimilative norm* for Black people to achieve (white) *personhood*. The cultural (rather than personal) impediment to sexual assimilation is evident in hypersexualized White-supremacist tropes, such as the Black male rapist and Black female jezebel (Curry, 2017; Brown et al., 2013; Lomax, 2018), which Black (subhuman) "men" and Black (subhuman) "women" are expected to redress by exhibiting "proper" (i.e., *white* disciplined) sexual behavior. Rarely do Whitepeople—including white sexuality professionals—question the racist sexual scripts that Whiteculture creates for themselves and others. Instead, most White sexuality professionals remain ignorant of the racist aspects of "positive" and "inclusive" discursive sexuality, which they in turn perpetuate.

Butler's (2016) question *Where are those of you who will support me now?* in the aforementioned quote is a refrain I am familiar with. Breaking with the solidarity of White Supremacy as a Whiteperson will get you accused of being a *defector* (i.e., woke and reverse racist) by other Whitepeople, as happened to me when I left the "safety" of my Whiteworld to *slum it*, according to my father, with Black and Brown friends in the aftermath of my sexual assault.

Our willingness to go it alone—*be* alone, *feel* alone, *do* alone—in the face of racial injustice is necessary race-based development for Whitepeople. Isolated antiracist acts, when performed solitarily *repeatedly* build momentum, creating solidarity *en masse* over space, place, and time. Additionally, as we will be reminded in Chapter 7, we are never truly alone.

Engaging in seemingly small isolated acts of antiracism allows Whitepeople to lean into the discomfort needed to become co-creative change agents, rather than *dysconscious performers* of whiteness and perpetrators of White-sex Supremacy. The *racist sexual caste system* built on conferred white power and maintained discursively through lack of critical examination can be dismantled through skillful means, starting with increased awareness of the indelible link between sex, gender, and race.

Radical Play Act

- **In the Theater of White-sex Supremacy, how are you a dysconscious performer of corporeal theatrics?**
  - **In social moments?**
  - **In sexually intimate moments?**

In the United States, "white" and "Black" are oppositional and hierarchical racial categories that apply to people. Whiteness and Blackness—meaning acts performed by white and Black people—are regulated by White Supremacy, such that race is performed through bodily acts (e.g., dress, grooming, gesture, and speech) (Ehlers, 2012), as well as racialized bodily trauma (Menakem, 2017). Because "race is not an intellectual or cognitive exercise, but a political and social construction that leaves scars on our body and nervous system" (Stern, 2021, para. 6) whiteness becomes a *cultural site* that decontextualizes space, place, and time, making splacetime a floating signifier for White-sex Supremacy.

> If something traumatic happens to you, the march of time will decontextualise [sic] it. Trauma in person over time can look like personality. Trauma, decontextualised [sic] over time in a family, can look like family traits. Trauma, decontextualised [sic] in a people, can look like culture.
>
> (Menakem, 2020, para. 43)

*White*culture is misperceived as *culture*, and racist sexual tropes are performed via White-sex scripting in splacetime.

White-Sex Scripting

The theatrical performance of White-sex Supremacy is the consequence of intergenerational scarring, activated nervous systems, and sexual scripting (introduced in Chapter 2) with an emphasis here on *racialized* sexual performativity. While sexual scripts can be misinterpreted as being predetermined *fixed* modes of sexual conduct, sexual script theory aims to elucidate sexual complexity (Gagnon & Simon, 1973; Gagnon, 1974/2004; Simon & Gagnon, 1986).

Gagnon and Simon (1973) acknowledge the confusion in their theory, including the limitation of the theatrical reference to *scripting:* while people *act* sexually, reference to the dramatic form is "more often than not . . . inappropriate" given that even conventional performances of sex are comprised of "a complicated set of layered symbolic meanings" (Gagnon & Simon, 1973, p. 23). This means that participants in the same sexual scenario may experience different sexual dramas at the same time (Gagnon & Simon, 1973; Gagnon, 1974/2004), illuminating sexual (and raced) synchronous nonsynchronicity.

Here, sexual script theory is referenced to show how corporeal theatrics is a dynamic performance (socioculturally predetermined and personally improvised) based on historical and emergent contexts of present absence (e.g., whiteness) and absent presence (e.g., Blackness) that occur in splacetime—on the stage of White-sex Theater.

Corporeal theatrics are on full display at the Cleveland Museum of Health (a cultural site) in the summer of 1945, as Norma and Normman, representing the statistical average (i.e., norm) of the (white) American young adult woman and man symbolize an emergent idealized modern white heterosexuality that Whitepeople mistake for *universal* sexuality, then and now, as if time stands still. Fast forward nearly eight decades, and the trauma of White-sex Supremacy is recognizable albeit in a different space, place, and time, like outside

Cup Foods in Minneapolis or in Central Park's Ramble. What is consistent is the cultural site of whiteness operating in splacetime.

> People have always taken space for granted. It is just emptiness, after all—a backdrop to everything else. Time, likewise, simply ticks on incessantly. But if physicists have learned anything from the long slog to unify their theories, it is that space and time form a system of such staggering complexity that it may defy our most ardent efforts to understand.
>
> (Musser, 2018, para. 1)

To comprehend how White Supremacy coopts splacetime, we must embrace the notion of "staggering complexity," or we will fail to interrogate its intricate apparatus.

White Splacetime

Both sexual scripting and performativity extend sex and sexuality beyond the boundaries of psyche and skin into the expansive and complex arena that is splacetime, shaped by hegemonic Whiteculture to become *white* splacetime, or what I refer to here as White-sex Theater.

Because sexual scripting and performativity require ongoing interpretation and negotiation (Jackson & Scott, 2010, p. 15), corporeal theatrics can be *re*scripted and *re*performed in the "arena of creative social initiative and symbolic action" (Gagnon, 1974/2004, p. xvi) by developing consciousness (Norbu, 1998) that is *also* present in splacetime. We review this in Chapter 7 with the intent to deconstruct White-sex Supremacy and (re)construct an emergent sexual freedom that occurs beyond the confines of sacrosanct *white* splacetime (i.e., White-sex Theater).

White Sex in the Ramble

On the morning of the day that George Floyd will die—on a Minneapolis city street in front of Cup Foods—Christian Cooper and Amy Cooper meet between 73rd and 79th Streets in New York City, in the 36-acre woodland section of Central Park known as the Ramble. Designed to mimic upstate New York with its forested Catskill and Adirondack mountains (my childhood stomping ground), the Ramble's dense fauna and wooded terrain is intended to mute the sights, sounds, and smells of the encroaching city that is just beyond its branches and park borders.

Manufactured Wildness

Halberstam (2020) describes wildness as "the absence of order, the entropic force of a chaos that constantly spins away from biopolitical attempts to manage life and bodies and desires" (p. 7). It is the opposite of the controlled environment of White Supremacy. "Wildness has no goal, no point of liberation that beckons off in the distance, no shape that must be assumed, no outcome that must be desired. Wildness, instead, disorders desire and desires disorder" (Halberstam, 2020, p. 7).

Landscape architect and Park co-designer, Frederick Law Olmsted, likens the Ramble to a "wild garden" meant to "evoke a place that appeared wild but was in fact heavily designed and managed" (Central Park Conservancy, 2021a., para. 4). The Ramble's *manufactured* wildness is the perfect location for White-sex Theater and the historical and unfolding drama of White-sex between the Coopers. With "opportunities for a more intimate and immersive experience" (Central Park Conservancy, 2021a., para. 4), the Ramble serves as a backdrop for how White-sex Supremacy manifests in white splacetime.

Racist Trope

That the Coopers meet in Central Park's Ramble is unremarkable, given where each of them lives in the city. The Ramble is where Christian Cooper frequently goes birding and Amy Cooper routinely walks her dog. The tenets of White-sex Supremacy also make the Ramble a *synchronous non-synchronistic* meeting place—haunted by the present absence of White Supremacy and the absent presence of its ghosts, most especially Threat of Rape. Together in the Ramble, the Coopers share the same historical moment but have different experiences of that moment based on their racialization, just as George Floyd and Derek Chauvin do later that day.

Sex Spot

Due to its thick vegetation, winding paths, and large boulders, the Ramble has been a venue for wanted and unwanted sexual encounters throughout the years. In the 1980s and 1990s, gay men frequented it for cruising (Fodero, 2012). Bird-watchers, like Christian Cooper, walk along its trails of littered condoms to spot some of the 210 species of birds that inhabit the park, such as northern cardinals, common yellow throats, and black-and-white warblers (Central Park Conservancy, 2021b). "Female bird-watchers report that they have sporadically glimpsed flashers, along with the flycatchers, grosbeaks and warblers that they have come to observe" (Fodero, 2012, para. 5).

The convergence of "idyllic" and "seedy" makes the Ramble the consummate backdrop for white fragility to encounter the Black male rapist trope, Threat of Rape, which is what occurs between Amy and Christian Cooper. Providing "the lexicon for massive systems of violence and the justification for the removal of Native and Black peoples, wildness . . . has historically been weaponized" (Halberstam, 2020, p. 7). The simulated wildness of the Ramble assists with the power-play performance of White-sex Supremacy, when Amy Cooper calls the police to falsely report Christian Cooper is assaulting her, while he is standing feet away from her in dense brush, asking that she adhere to the park's policy and leash her dog. Instead, Amy Cooper unleashes her whiteness. As Christian Cooper records her on his cell phone, her racial entitlement and white fragility are on full display. She follows through on her threat to Christian Cooper: *I'm going to tell them there's an African American man threatening my life* (Wong, 2021). Public backlash is swift: Amy Cooper loses her job, her dog, and to an outraged public, her dignity.

What occurs in the Ramble between the Coopers on the day George Floyd will die are the corporeal theatrics of White-sex Supremacy, and the cooption of splacetime by whiteness causing dislocation, dismemberment, and mourning for Black bodies—a tragically literal manifestation for George Floyd.

Dislocation: Mourning Home

Racial mourning centers on dislocation: loss of origin, loss of consent. Whitesettlers in America do not mourn home, whereas dispossessed African Americans and Black people often do. Whitepeople have the luxury of moving through splacetime with ease, as entitled FreeWhitePeople, like Amy Cooper in the Ramble, and Derek Chauvin in front of Cup Foods. White Supremacy creates:

> a context [of mourning] that does not privilege one's deepest desire to return home and inhabit one's own agency and body, but instead triggers disembodiment, making certain meanings out of Black bodies, minds, and spirits that fulfill the intentions of the racist capitalist imagination.
>
> (Owens, 2020, p. 245)

Lama Dawa Tarchin Phillips (2020) refers to this as "the amputated self" (p. 85), severed from aspects of identity experienced as mental, emotional, spiritual, and physical dislocation—bringing "isolation, meaninglessness, loneliness, and depression" (p. 86). Dislocation is severance from *home*—both a physical location and psychological state.

Yetunde (2020) describes this as being "invisibilized" by the community to which you are supposed to belong (p. 103). Selassie (2020) confides how loss of home causes her to turn away from herself, yet another traumatic form of severance. The *language of loss* by people of color includes *disconnection, amputation, isolation, loneliness, invisibility*—an erasure that is experienced as *splatial* dislocation (i.e., separation from space and place) and psychological dissociation. In each of their experiences of mourning, there are also echoes of resilience and perseverance—capacities Whitepeople need to acquire to address racial stress. To do so, we must first develop outrage.

Rage and Outrage

The antithesis of white fragility, it seems to me, is *rage*. Not having it, but holding it for others. *Othered* others. Particularly for those who are Black in our field and in our lives, because rage is arguably a sane and adaptive response to racism. White fragility, on the other hand, is a maladaptive response. *Out*rage is far more useful.

Distinguishing between rage and outrage is critical, given that rage is the appropriate response of those who are unduly affected by the injustice of race and the psychic and social burden of negotiating displacement in splacetime that occurs as Black people maneuver within the context of White-sex Theater to survive. Rage manifests inwardly, coalescing around anger and/or fury over injustice(s) perpetrated against oneself, whereas outrage manifests *out*wardly. It refuses to accept untenable conditions. Outrage seeks justice as the remedy. White fragility is the reactive state in which the slightest hint of racial stress becomes intolerable, and the Whiteperson caves to emotional frailty and fear. Instead of building capacity for discomfort, we collapse under duress. White fragility is more closely aligned with flee and freeze responses of the nervous system, than with fight. As Whitepeople, we need to learn how to fight for *freedom from* versus *freedom to* (as detailed in Chapter 3) where freedom from sexual violence, discrimination, coercion experience supersedes white sexual liberation.

Black Rage

Racial melancholia as conceived by David Eng and Shinhee Han (Eng, 2010; Eng & Han, 2019) provides a plausible context for—and possible precursor to—Black rage. As a theoretical framework meant to "analyze the ungrievable losses associated with everyday experiences of immigration, assimilation, and racialization for Asian immigrations and their second-generation offspring" (Eng, 2010, p. 150), racial melancholia may be useful for more thoroughly understanding the effects of Black-body erasure. Contesting Freud's distinction between melancholia and mourning—the former of which he viewed as an unceasing pathological disposition, Eng and Han (2019) characterize racial melancholia as an adaptive daily toggle between mourning and melancholia—a persistent negotiation due to social and psychic conflict not psychological damage (Eng, 2010; Eng & Han, 2019).

In *Disidentifications: Queers of Color and the Performance of Politics*, José Esteban Muñoz similarly proposes that melancholia is not a pathological condition but an everyday necessity for survival, predicated on mourning. *Mourning* is defined as the *cognitive* experience of loss, whereas *grief* is its *emotional and physiological* expression (Bridges, 2001). Mourning, melancholia, and grief are the experiences of racialized erasure—the foundation for Black rage. Black rage is the justifiable consequence of White Supremacy that Whitepeople need to get comfortable with in order to develop skillful outrage as antiracist allies.

White Outrage

In the wake of George Floyd's murder, Black Lives Matter became a slogan of outrage for many of my white friends and colleagues. Yet white outrage is only beneficial if it simultaneously carries the capacity to hold Black mourning, melancholia, and grief that is *consequential rage*. Outrage without this foundation is too fragile to do much good. In *Eloquent Rage: A Black Feminist Discovers Her Superpower*, Brittney Cooper reminds us that "individual transformation is neither a substitute for nor a harbinger of structural transformation" (Cooper, 2018, p. 115). Still, Whitepeople building personal capacity for outrage is a necessary step on the Yellow Brick Road to reveal what is behind the White Curtain.

Gianna

The text I receive from my Black stepdaughter, Gianna, reads in part:

> *My go to response when I'm upset with someone and they've hurt me is to stop talking to them for my own protection but I realize that it hurts people and is not my true intention. I've been keeping my feelings toward you in a locked box.*

I had failed Gianna *before* George Floyd was murdered and Black Lives Matter became a slogan in our collective consciousness, but the increasing visibility of anti-Blackness (on TV, social media, and in the streets) during a global pandemic compounded my failure. Gianna was upset with me for my being insensitive when her father was facing unexpected surgery and I worried aloud about the financial implications for our family. My indoctrination into white neoliberalism caused me to value money more than my partner's health in a stressful moment. At the time, I apologized for my insensitivity, understanding it was (partially) caused by stress. However, what I failed to recognize at that moment was the broader racial context of my insensitivity and its impact on the bodies and hearts of those I love.

Radical Play Act

- **Who have you harmed with your racial insensitivity, your Whiteness?**
- **What discursive tactics did you use:**

  - **Were you dismissive of race by employing universalist language? (e.g., All Lives Matter. We Are One. There is one race: the "human" race.)**
  - **Were you race-evasive, pretending that race is not present in intimate moments?**

I was optimistic enough to believe I could repair the hurt and lessen the increasing distance between Gianna and me, given the role utopian principles play in antiracist work; a large-scale example being the American Abolitionist Movement (c. 1830–1870) with its utopian goal to end slavery, which it ultimately did. Utopian principles are necessary for smaller, more localized antiracist initiatives too.

Utopian Dreams

The sidewalks in Chittenango, New York, 20 minutes from where I grew up, are painted yellow to honor the birthplace of writer L. Frank Baum, who died in 1919, 20 years before his *The Wonderful Wizard of Oz* became a motion picture. This is an example of how the fruits of our sentience may manifest long after we are gone, making utopian dreams worth striving for. Utopian principles are idealistic *and* practical; large and small: from abolishing slavery to baking brownies for Ben and Jerry's Ice Cream.

Chocolate Brownies

Utopian principles were embraced by Greyston's founder, Bernie Glassman, a former aeronautical engineer turned Buddhist monk, who told an audience at Naropa that his vision was a local yet bold one: to *eradicate homelessness* in Yonkers, New York. This utopian vision inspired him to take the *practical step* of forming a bakery in 1982 to "bake brownies to put people to work" which is the company's slogan (Greyston Bakery, 2021). As New York's first certified B Corporation, Greyston remains committed to its open-door hiring policy (i.e., anyone willing to work is given the opportunity, regardless of education, homelessness, drug use, and incarceration). "There are no background checks and no prescreening of any kind—when a position becomes available, the next person on the waiting list gets it, no questions asked" (Greyston Bakery, 2021). This example of *utopian dreaming* suggests that transformative social change is achievable. Eradicating White-sex Supremacy is the utopian vision we must strive for, even in seemingly inconsequential ways, given its consequential harm to Black bodies.

Herz and Johansson (2015) similarly assert that *utopian strategies* can be used for deconstructing heteronormativity and its whiteness by implementing *bottom-up* and *top-down* utopian approaches.

Bottom Up, Top Down

The *bottom-up* utopian strategy favors equal rights for all regardless of sexual preference, with its utopian vision aimed at creating an inclusive sexually liberated society, whereas the *top-down* strategy promotes the transgression of intimate relationships and conventional lifestyles toward dismantling and overhauling society's fundamental structures and institutions. The bottom-up approach underestimates how sexuality is shaped by history and socialization, whereas the top-down approach emphasizes a systemic view, but does so at the expense of individual lives. Therefore, Herz and Johansson (2015) argue for a combined approach.

The bottom-up/top-down utopian approach allows for a revision of entrenched normativities, starting with individuals and kinship systems (e.g., families, communities) centering on everyday lives, personal agency, and social practices so that local and personal differences can be contextualized without negating global and structural influences. The "potential space of reflexivity and political change involves both subjects and structures . . . creating alliances between different social movements, the ultimate aim being the end of discrimination, sexual oppression, and harassment" (Herz & Johansson, 2015, p. 1019).

I suggest initiating a bottom-up/top-down utopian approach by engaging *playmind* (discussed in the final chapter) for effectuating change based on embodied perspective-taking, and mindfulness-based awareness practice.

7   Cultivating Playmind

Because "everything relies on everything else in the cosmos in order to manifest—whether a star, a cloud, a flower, a tree, or you and me" we are interconnected (Hanh, 2017a, p. 14). Nevertheless, we convince ourselves otherwise, living in deluded and painful states of separation (e.g., disembodied, imprisoned, warring). To accentuate our interconnection Thich Nhat Hanh, the Vietnamese Zen Buddhist monk and revered spiritual teacher, who died during the writing of this book at the age of 95, on January 22, 2022, created the verb *inter-be* over 30 years ago to underscore that we *cannot be* by our lonesome. It is not how we survive, let alone thrive. We exist and develop interconnectedly. Quite simply, he says: "We inter-are" (Hanh, 2017a, p. 14). Our lives are not solitary acts but rather intersecting currents in a complex system with consequences. There is cause and effect, what Buddhists call *karma*.

Writer James Baldwin (1976/2011) acknowledges interbeingness in *The Devil Finds Work*:

> To encounter oneself is to encounter the other: and this is love. If I know that my soul trembles, I know that yours does, too: and if I can respect this, both of us can live. Neither of us, truly, can live without the other: a statement which would not sound so banal if one were not so endlessly compelled to repeat it, and act on that belief.
>
> (pp. 125–126)

The final chapter of this book is a reaffirmation of the fundamental principle and practice to *inter-be*. It is the foundation of antiracist work, and what Whitepeople often dysconsciously ignore to retain their racial comfort and power.

Interbeingness

Referencing the work of Lewis Thomas, a biologist, Hanh (2017b) describes *interbeing* as a symbiotic process:

> Our human bodies are "shared, rented, and occupied" by countless other tiny organisms, without whom we couldn't "move a muscle, drum a finger,

DOI: 10.4324/9781003190035-8

or think a thought." Our body is a community, and the trillions of non-human cells in our body are even more numerous than the human cells. Without them, we could not be here in this moment. Without them, we wouldn't be able to think, to feel, or to speak. There are, [Lewis] says, no solitary beings. The whole planet is one giant, living, breathing cell with all its working parts linked in symbiosis.

(para. 3)

That our body is *more community than identity* (e.g., male, female, Black, white, young, old) emphasizes symbiosis, which we learned in Chapter 2 is an interactive long-term relationship between two different species, with distinct outcomes to host and symbiont: *benefit–harm, benefit–neutral,* and *benefit–benefit,* corresponding with *segregationist, assimilative,* and *antiracist* ideologies and practices (Kendi, 2016).

Based on mutuality and interdependency, the benefit–benefit symbiotic practice of antiracism is predicated on *interbeingness* according to Hanh (2017a, 2017b), *love* according to Baldwin (1976/2011), *pleasure* according to brown (2019), and our "open and fearless . . . capacity for joy" according to Lorde (1984/2007, p. 56). These qualities (i.e., interbeingness, love, pleasure, and fearless joy) invite what Kyabje Dungse Thinley Norbu (1998), a revered Tibetan Buddhist teacher, calls *playmind,* which is how we best *dance* with the illusory nature of our phenomenal existence—by cultivating a calm, vast, open, and playful state of mind.

Playmind

Playmind is a playful state of consciousness that reenergizes rather than drains us: "Serious mind is always exhausted, but playmind always has energy" (Norbu, n.d.; Embodiment Matters, 2020). Playmind, with a foundation in sympathetic joy, is the practical utopian principle we must cultivate for antiracist work. It incorporates the bottom-up/top-down utopian approach introduced in the previous chapter by joining interbeingness with the immediacy of the present moment, exemplified in the state of compersion.

Sympathetic Joy

Compersion, a term frequently referenced within consensually non-monogamous polyamorous communities, is derived from the Buddhist concept of *sympathetic joy,* described as the experience of ecstatic delight in seeing close others happy (Fern, 2020; Hardy & Easton, 2019; Veaux & Rickert, 2014). Delighting in the happiness of others expands our capacity for joy—for others and also ourselves—as we open to new vistas, beyond limiting binaries and normative thinking.

We-ness

Mutuality (our *we*-ness) and *interdependency* (the ways in which the self is changed by close others) are key facets of intimacy (Miller, 2022) and the hallmark of interbeingness. Like it or not, White Supremacy *intimately* conjoins Black and white bodies through intergenerational (racial and sexual) trauma, even as our reactivity to this suffering causes us to separate, segregate, and remain "othered" to each other. As stated in Chapter 1, being American is being biracial—both Black and white—it is also denying "our deep biracial genesis" (Hale, 1998, p. 3).

The genesis of our biracial existence creates sinews—binding present to past, like muscle to bone—through the haunting legacy of rape, compelling our desire to flee from White Supremacy and our interbeingness. Like fibrous connective tissue, the suffering of White Supremacy yokes us even as we seek "liberation from the dictates of that *we*" (Coates, 2018, para. 29). In "Kanye West in the Age of Donald Trump," Coates (2018) reflects on how both Kanye and Michael Jackson, as Black performers, seek liberation from the boundedness of we:

> When Jackson sang and danced, when West samples or rhymes, they are tapping into a power formed under all the killing, all the beatings, all the rape and plunder that made America. The gift can never wholly belong to a singular artist, free of expectation and scrutiny, because the gift is no more solely theirs than the suffering that produced it.
>
> (para. 28)

Attempts to *unyoke* ourselves from a history and present steeped in White Supremacy result in corporeal theatrics, as we learned in Chapter 6. In this way, Michael Jackson's nose is a *national symbol* of White-body Supremacy, demonstrating the lengths to which a Black body will go to resurrect itself from erasure by White Supremacy (Coates, 2018). Whitepeople also augment their bodies to appeal to White-supremacist standards of beauty. Feigning fragility is another way that we, as Whitepeople, attempt to escape.

In a neoliberal context, interbeing is recognized and valued but only insomuch as it does not impede individualistic pursuits of pleasure, which form the basis of sex positivity, including its promise of sexual liberation (more than freedom). For this reason, Whitepeople must develop playmind alongside the increasing capacity for discomfort. Here, I have suggested that we do this by engaging in Radical Play Acts to transform knowledge into wisdom, and meaning into sense.

Crazy Wisdom

I credit Chögyam Trungpa, a preeminent teacher of Tibetan Buddhism and Naropa's founder, for the concept of radical play given its association with *crazy wisdom*, a term used to describe a method of teaching and spiritual practice that he was known for. Crazy wisdom often appears symptomatic of "madness" or "mental illness" to the unaware observer (DiValerio, 2011; Kottler, 2005). Also referred to as *divine madness*, crazy wisdom is considered to be an alternative state of consciousness derived from spiritual or religious ecstasy (DiValerio, 2011; Kottler, 2005). This *mad*, or eccentric, behavior can also be understood as performative, "a strategic, purposeful activity, rather than being the byproduct of a state of enlightenment" (DiValerio, 2011, p. ii). This interpretation is consistent with W. Puck Brecher's (2013) findings in *The Aesthetics of Strangeness: Eccentricity and Madness in Early Modern Japan*, which concludes "the eccentric, mad, and strange are moral exemplars, paragons of virtue, and shining hallmarks of modern consciousness" (p. xx; Kottler, 2005) capable of generating aesthetic, intellectual, and social heterodoxies that impact society. As a practice of crazy wisdom, radical play is a revelatory gesture that pierces—like punctum—offering penetrating insight. Hence, the invitation to radically play to unsettle ourselves and our whiteness.

Writing Red

During a writing workshop at Naropa, my colleague Bhanu Kapil, an experimental writer and poet, instigated radical play by placing red-colored ice cubes in the shape of hearts onto our upward-facing palms so we could: *Write with our paws, uncensored*. Our hands, bodies, canvases and the floor were covered with red food dye, as our minds popped out of habitual ways of thinking and writing. After writing *red*—the color of sexuality, transgression, blood, and love—participants in Bhanu's workshop commented on its unsettling yet playful effects, making radical play conducive to our work as antiracist sexuality professionals through the cultivation of an open and curious playmind. As Whitesettlers, we need to be unsettled in our bodies *and* minds through activities like writing red.

Aimless Wandering

I felt consistently *unsettled* as a graduate student in the Contemplative Psychotherapy program at Naropa, with its "under the microscope" cohort model, that taught me firsthand (like it or not) the value of radical play. One of the radical play activities I was introduced to early on was *aimless wandering*. This deliberate goalless meandering into uncertainty—referred to elsewhere as *flaneuring* with its queer history and connection to white dandyism, including its asexual, homosexual, and effeminate attributes (Owen, 2019)—requires that we move into space *literally*, to intentionally yet pointless wander about, like an old white dandy:

> who would idly stroll through the streets of a city carefully observing his everyday surroundings and finding beauty in what many would consider

the mundane. The kind of strolling these early flaneurs did was always done with a romantic mind-set—or a greater focus on *finding meaning in the cracks* [emphasis added] in the street than getting somewhere specific.

(Owen, 2019, p. 2)

Notably, moving into space—into every nook and cranny—is how whiteness strengthens its up-power. Thus, I posit that we wander there, too; getting lost intentionally, with attentiveness to all we encounter. Becoming at times confused. When we cling to our cherished certainty, we foreclose on failure, mishaps, and mistakes, which we learned through the "queer art of failure" (Halberstam, 2011) addressed in Chapter 3, can be portals to new ways of *doing* and *being*, informing ethical behavior.

Radical Play Act

- **Assume the nineteenth-century sport of a white Parisian male dandy, and flaneur:**
  - **Like you did in Chapter 2 by identifying objects of whiteness in your home, notice evidence of whiteness outside.**
  - **Find meaning in the (literal and figurative) *cracks* of White Supremacy.**
  - **What did you notice? How did you make meaning?**

Unsettling Actor, Ally, Accomplice

Johnathan Osler (n.d.) introduces gradations of unsettling White Supremacy by distinguishing between *actors, allies*, and *accomplices* in the guide he developed for Whitepeople (edited by BIPOC).

Actors

Actors are spectators in the drama of White Supremacy who remain settled and comfortable in their whiteness, maintaining the racial status quo, rather than disrupting it. Actors fail to name and/or challenge White Supremacy and its pillars, impeding progress toward social justice.

Allies

Allies act as more verb than noun; committed to challenging spaces dominated by Whitepeople, they begin to unsettle. Importantly, the term "ally" is not a self-recognized proclamation but granted by those who are oppressed. Allies understand and challenge institutionalized racism and White Supremacy. Allies disrupt and educate about splacetime dominated by Whiteness.

Accomplices

Accomplices are exemplars of unsettling, relying on meaningful endurance. They actively and routinely address White Supremacy and racism head-on, directly challenging racist structures, policies, and people. Accomplices act on the principle of interbeing, whether they refer to it as such or not. Their motivation hinges on the interconnectedness of all beings (and the planet) instead of personal motivation (e.g., shame, guilt, and fear) by knowing that our *freedom to* is bound to our *freedom from*. They establish and maintain trust through accountability, acting in concert with others not in isolation. They listen actively and take direction from BIPOC leaders.

Antiracist

Antiracism pushes unsettling even further. The book jacket for *How to Be an Antiracist* by Ibram X. Kendi (2019) says it best: "Antiracism is a transformative concept that reorients and reenergizes the conversation about racism—and, even more fundamentally, points us toward liberating new ways of thinking about ourselves and each other." This is what playmind—via Radical Play Acts—attempts to do. Without it, liberatory sexual discourse is overly serious and propagates *white freedom* instead of freedom for all.

White Freedom

Discourses of white freedom have grown louder and more insistent as privacy rights are rescinded (e.g., Roe vs. Wade) and racist-motivated hate crimes (e.g., mass shootings) become commonplace.

> White freedom, freedom without consequence, freedom without criticism, freedom to be proud and ignorant; freedom to profit off a people in one moment and abandon them in the next; a Stand Your Ground freedom, freedom without responsibility, without hard memory; a Monticello without slavery, a Confederate freedom, the freedom of John C. Calhoun, not the freedom of Harriet Tubman, which calls you to risk your own; not the freedom of Nat Turner, which calls you to give even more, but a conqueror's freedom, freedom of the strong built on antipathy or indifference to the weak, the freedom of rape buttons, pussy grabbers, and *fuck you anyway, bitch*; freedom of oil and invisible wars, the freedom of suburbs drawn with red lines, the white freedom of Calabasas.
>
> (Coates, 2018, para. 29)

In *On Freedom: Four Songs of Care and Constraint*, Maggie Nelson (2021) makes a case for rearticulating and reclaiming freedom without phallocentric use of time and reasoning focused on *future achievement*. Instead,

Nelson (2021) acknowledges that freedom is "an unending *present practice,* something already going on" (p. 6). Serra (2019) similarly imagines sexual freedom as a communal practice of justice, starting with imagining futures *beyond oppression* by working actively in Here and Now:

> We need to start by listening. We need to acknowledge that a lot of work has been done in these spaces, especially by marginalized people, and we need to lift those voices up. We need new questions. It's not sufficient to simply ask what we want for ourselves or what it means to be in a body without sexual shame. We must ask: what do we need, collectively, to heal and reimagine. Because sexuality is at one both utterly individual and communal. It is how we relate with ourselves and with the culture at large.
>
> (p. 214)

Playmind as Presence

As white sexuality professionals, we must recognize how easily white fragility coopts us and the splacetime we inhabit, as it did on Memorial Day 2020—to Derek Chauvin on the sidewalk in front of Cup Foods and in Central Park's Ramble to Amy Cooper. Unlike playmind, which is expansive, white fragility constricts consciousness due to fear. We revert to habituated thinking and behavior. Therefore, it is critical to develop playmind through *presence* and the capacity to *suspend reactivity*. Through mindful suspension, we can recognize and disarm white fragility, rather than act upon it.

Seeing Our Seeing

Presence as direct awareness deepens our capacity to suspend (Senge et al., 2004) requiring that we interrogate our assumptions—by *seeing our seeing*—instead of accepting reality as we have been socialized (Senge et al., 2004). Seeing our seeing suspends our habituated thinking and reactivity, fostering the reflexivity necessary for developing diverse and inclusive sexuality that is neither racist nor race-evasive.

Theory U

Considered the "core capacity needed to access the field of the future," the Theory U model was created to access *presence* (Senge et al., 2004, p. 13; Scharmer, 2019). Presence facilitates fresh insights and innovative responsiveness rather than familiarity and habituated reactivity.

A pause is inserted at the top of the (figurative) U (on the left-hand side) to interrupt the propensity to solve a problem quickly, or linearly. The pause enables a vertical drop into uncertainty and not-knowing. Verticality invites the processes of *suspending, redirecting, letting go,* and *letting come* to "sense an emerging future" (Senge et al., p. 84). Presence propels us into the immediacy and intimacy of the current moment.

Five Eye Practices

In the chapter "Addressing White Fragility through Mindfulness-Based Inquiry in Sexuality Leadership" in the *Handbook of Sexuality Leadership: Inspiring Community Engagement, Social Empowerment, and Transformational Influence*, my colleague, Satori Madrone, and I (Clements & Madrone, 2020) introduced the Five Eye Practices, developed by Barbara Dilley, Professor Emeritus of Dance at Naropa University, as an embodied method for decentering whiteness. I incorporate it here to address interrogating White-sex Supremacy from a state of wholeness. Originally designed for *Naked Face*, a museum installation in 1996, the Five Eye Practices elicit *embodied perspective-taking*, with practices that include

(1) Closed Eyes
(2) Infant Eyes
(3) Peripheral Seeing
(4) Looking Between Things
(5) Direct Looking

(Dilley, 2015, pp. 123–124)

To these (with Barbara's permission), I have added a sixth: *Seeing Behind*, which I insert between practices four and five.

As Barthes (1980) suggests, fresh perspective-taking alters *seer* and *seen*. The Five Eye Practices interrupt our dualistic meaning-making (i.e., good–bad, us–them) as "we shift from looking 'out at the world' from the viewpoint of a detached [white] observer to looking from 'inside' what is being observed" (Senge et al., 2004, p. 41). The Five Eye Practices disrupt the false separation between self and Other, redirecting us toward interbeingness.

Closed Eyes

Closing our eyes initiates self-reflection. The activity of the outer world recedes as our focus turns inward, noticing physiological and emotional experience (e.g., sweaty palms, shallow breathing, frustration, disappointment). With eyes closed, we relax and refresh to perceive more fully. Here, we release our racialized fear, anxiety, and fragility.

Infant Eyes

Eyes open softly to gaze at our surroundings. Eyes lead, head and spine follow. Infant eyes invite us to see anew, *before naming*. For example, rather than *naming color* (e.g., blue or green), we notice hues, the interplay of shadow and light. Here, as Whitesettlers, we resist our compulsion to *know, name* and *judge*. Curiosity becomes key.

Peripheral Seeing

Here, we see from the corner of our eyes instead of straight ahead. If we out-stretch our arms (in the shape of a T) while looking forward and wiggling our fingers, we locate the periphery. In this way, we begin to decenter whiteness by noticing the margins, given that what is beyond our direct seeing is often ignored and undervalued.

Looking Between Things

Looking between emphasizes the importance of liminality. For example, rather than focusing on the branches of a tree, we look at the sky between the branches. This practice accentuates background rather than foreground. The absent presence of BIPOC and the omnipresence of whiteness are revealed.

Seeing Behind

Seeing behind is the eye practice I added to increase awareness of our back body. Depending on our social locations (i.e., privileged or oppressed), we may be more or less aware, more or less secure or troubled by what might be happening behind us. Seeing behind stretches our perceptual circumference to that of a wise old owl *Who-Who* sees 270 degrees.

LITTLE DISCIPLINES

Dilley (2015) explains that the first four eye practices are "little disciplines" preparing us to look directly. Without them, direct looking is unformed (too casual, even lazy) causing us to miss details, nuance, and the fullness of all that is there. Having engaged the previous eye practices, we can now look directly to (re)perceive *What Is* (coming full circle from the start of this book) including what is beyond sociocultural limitations, so that direct looking becomes imbued with the immediacy of the moment and utopian potential of Black Futurities.

Direct Looking

Looking directly allows us to observe "small, intimate aspects about what [we] are seeing . . . patterns in the wood on the floor, the way a light fixture is connected to the ceiling, how leaves on a tree outside the window move in the breeze" (Dilley, 2015, p. 124). Direct looking enables us to re-engage White Supremacy with precision and spacious panoramic awareness.

I learned the Five Eye Practices from Barbara Dilley years ago at a faculty development workshop at Naropa, before she wrote her book *This Very Moment: Teaching, Thinking, Dancing*, which contains this and other playmind activities. I am fortunate to work at a university that centers mindfulness, giving me access to ancient and contemporary awareness practices. It does not, however, prevent us from reenacting White Supremacy as a predominantly white institution. What it does do is encourage us to *stay in relationship* with each other, cultivating intimacy of presence during difficult encounters and conflictual moments. *Staying*, I have found, is the most worthwhile yet difficult relational practice I know, and critical for white sexuality professionals to develop.

Conclusion
Shall We Stay?

Although I do not know to what degree, I am certain this writing project has failed. Surely, it has failed to produce the revolutionary counterculture change our field needs. I am not lamenting but *stating a fact*, which has become an undervalued pastime of White America (if ever it was one). (re)Learning facticity as Whitepeople starts with *calling out* (forget the courtesy of *calling in*) *What Is*. Most certainly, what is *white*.

In (progressive) Whiteculture, positivity manifests *nicely*. Dresses up in earnest. Ready to *be* good, *do* good. As Whitepeople, our be-gooder/do-gooder mentality is an obstacle to manifesting transformational change because it bypasses emotional discomfort: rushes in to fix, which is often as much an avoidance tactic for difficult emotions as it is a desire to help. We cannot avoid White Supremacy and its racist sexualization. It stares us in the face. Daily. If we just look in the mirror, we will see it staring back.

I have attempted to show how White-sex Supremacy functions in splace-time, (re)perceiving it queerly (with Radical Play Acts) toward ending our corporeal theatrics that make us complicit in the erasure of Black bodies and sexualities. To do this, I have advocated that we recognize how discursive sex positivity serves as a smokescreen for white sexuality professionals to hide behind, requiring that we confront our discursive habits of mind, which embrace sex positivity without critical examination. As a cursory invitation to inclusion, sex positivity reinforces sexual racism, upholding White-sex Supremacy.

Menakem (2020) urges Whitepeople to create community and culture that effectuate change, rather than self-care routines, which in a *McMindful*-based Whiteculture like ours is essential, given that "betterment" (including sexual betterment) is code for eugenicist thinking. Our *intent* to be antiracist as white sexuality professionals does little to effect cultural transformation when our intention is paired with dysconscious racism. Rather than failing queerly, we fail to be critical thinkers.

> The point of this language of "intention" and "personal responsibility" is broad exoneration. Mistakes were made. Bodies were broken. People were

DOI: 10.4324/9781003190035-9

enslaved. We meant well. We tried our best. "Good intention" is a hall pass through history, a sleeping pill that ensures the Dream.

(Coates, 2015, p. 33)

The Dream Coates (2015) is referring to is White Futurity, which I encountered at the age of 3, when I moved into the house my parents built at 2 Future Street in a white borough that befittingly remains a Dead End. To awake from the Dream of White Supremacy, Coates (2015) urges Black bodies to "forget about intentions" given that "what any institutions, or their agents, 'intend' for you is secondary" (p. 33). "Learn to play defense," he urges, "keep your eyes on the body" (Coates, 2015, p. 33). While Black people *embody* Whitepeople *disembody*, becoming reactive and fragile—ill-equipped to tackle the complexities of racism, let alone move the needle toward cultural transformation. By valorizing white consciousness, we shift from bodily to discursive identity as Whitepeople, the basis of dysconscious racism.

At the end (like at the beginning) of this book, I desire to take flight (as a bird or winged angel) toward realizing my childhood dream to jump from the roof of my parents' house of my own volition and *fly*. Far. Far. Away. After all, I remain white, socialized to believe that the Dream of White Supremacy is a fact, disconnecting rather than binding us through the aesthetics of representation and difference, as if Us versus Them supersedes our We-ness.

Whitepeople's task is to *remember* our interbeingness like an act of mourning, which remembering is. Remembering *to breathe* and ask queer questions, such as *What do we know about dismemberment?* (Hopefully, we know something now.)

Despite our collective Dream, and our impulse as Whitepeople to *fly far away* from our racial responsibilities, our task is to remain fully present in the Here and Now, with a final:

Radical Play Act

• **How long are you willing to stay?**

As long as it takes? Anything less is a sign of your white privilege.

References

Ahmed, S. (2006). *Queer phenomenology: Orientations, objects, others.* Duke University Press.

Alexander, M. (2011). *The new Jim Crow: Mass incarceration in the age of colorblindness.* The New Press.

Allred, M. K. (2017). *Weimar cinema, embodiment, and historicity: Cultural memory and the historical films of Ernst Lubitsch.* Taylor & Francis.

American Psychiatric Association. (2013). *The diagnostic and statistical manual of mental health disorders* (5th ed.). American Psychiatric Association.

Anderson, B., Narum, A., & Wolf, J. L. (2019). Expanding the understanding of the categories of dysconscious racism. *The Educational Forum, 83*(1), 4–12. https://doi.org/10.1080/00131725.2018.1505015

Arao, B., & Clemens, K. (2013). From safe spaces to brave spaces: A new way to frame dialogue around diversity and social justice. In L. M. Landreman (Ed.), *The art of effective facilitation: Reflections from social justice educators* (pp. 134–150). Stylus.

Baldwin, J. (1953). Strangers in the village. *Harper's Magazine.*

Baldwin, J. (2011). *The devil finds work.* Vintage Books. (Original work published 1976)

Barker, K. K. (2014). Mindfulness meditation: Do-it-yourself medicalization of every moment. *Social Science Medicine, 106*, 168–176. https://doi.orgd/10.1016/j.socscimed.2014.01.024

Barker, M., & Hancock, J. (2019). Sex positive, sex-negative, or sex critical. In A. Gabosch & J. Shub (Eds.), *Sex positive now* (pp. 23–26). Sexy Activist Publishing.

Barstow, C. (2021). On the right use of power with Cedar Barstow [Video file]. *YouTube. Shambhala Mountain Center.* www.youtube.com/watch?v=SjMMf5lWpag

Barstow, C., & Feldman, R. R. (2013). *Living in the power zone: How right use of power can transform your relationships.* Many Realms.

Barthes, R. (1980). *Camera lucida: Reflections on photography* (R. Howard, Trans.). Hill and Wang.

Basson, R. (2000). The female sexual response: A different model. *Journal of Sex & Marital Therapy, 26*(1), 51–65.

Basson, R. (2003). Biopsychosocial models of women's sexual response: Applications to management of "desire disorders." *Sexual and Relationship Therapy, 18*(1), 107–115. https://doi.org/10.1080/1468199031000061308

Beard, G. M. (1880). *A practical treatise on nervous exhaustion (neurasthenia).* G. P. Putnam's Sons.

Beard, G. M. (1881). *American nervousness.* G. P. Putnam's Sons.

Beard, G. M. (1884). *Sexual neurasthenia.* E. B. Treat.

Bellerose, C. (2018). On the lived, imagined body: A phenomenological practice of somatic architecture. *Phenomenology & Practice, 12*(1), 57–71.

Bem, S. L. (1993). *The lenses of gender: Transforming the debate on sexual inequality.* Yale University Press.

Bloch, E. (1977). Nonsynchronism and the obligation to its dialectics (M. Ritter, Trans.). *New German Critique, 11,* 22–38. (Original work published 1932)

Bloch, E. (1991). *Heritage of our time* (N. Plaice & S. Plaice, Trans.). Polity Press. (Original work published in 1935)

Bologna, C. (2018, August 9). Why the phrase 'pull yourself up by the bootstraps' is nonsense. *Huffington Post.* www.huffpost.com/entry/pull-yourself-up-by-your-bootstraps-nonsense_n_5b1ed024e4b0bbb7a0e037d4

Borren, M. (2019, June 26). The spatial phenomenology of white embodiment. *Locus.* https://locus.ou.nl/locus-dossier-het-lichaam/the-spatial-phenomenology-of-white-embodiment-marieke-borren/

Brecher, W. P. (2013). *The aesthetics of strangeness: Eccentricity and madness in early modern Japan.* University of Hawaii Press.

Bridges, W. (2001). *The way of transition: Embracing life's most difficult moments.* DaCapo Press.

Bridges, W. (2004). *Transitions: Making sense of life's changes* (Rev. ed.). DeCapo Lifelong Books. (Original work published 1979)

British Broadcasting Corporation. (2016, October, 9). U.S. Election: Full transcript of Donald Trump's obscene videotape. *BBC News.* www.bbc.com/news/election-us-2016-37595321

Brown, A. (2019). *Pleasure activism: The politics of feeling good.* AK Press.

Brown, D. L., White-Johnson, R. L., & Griffin-Fennell, F. (2013). Breaking the chains: Examining the endorsement of modern jezebel images and racial-ethnic esteem among African American women. *Culture, Health & Sexuality, 15*(5), 525–539.

Brown, Y. (2008). Ghosts in the Canadian multicultural machine. A tale of the absent presence of black people. *Journal of Black Studies, 38*(3), 374–387.

Burnes, T. R., Singh, A. A., & Witherspoon, R. G. (2017). An introduction to the major contribution. *The Counseling Psychologist, 45*(4), 470–486.

Butler, J. (1999). *Gender trouble: Feminism and the subversion of identity.* Routledge. (Original work published 1990)

Butler, J. (2011). *Bodies that matter.* Routledge. (Original work published 1993)

Butler, J. (2016). In terms of performance: Performativity. In S. Jackson & P. Marincola (Eds.), *The Pew center for arts & heritage and the University of California, Berkeley.* http://intermsofperformance.site/keywords/performativity/judith-butler

Caldwell, C., & Leighton, L. B. (2018). *Oppression and the body: Roots, resistance, and resolutions.* North Atlantic Books.

Camara, B. (2005). The falsity of Hegel's theses on Africa. *Journal of Black Studies, 36*(1), 82–96.

Carroll, L. (2019). *Through the looking glass.* (Original work published 1871)

Carter, J. (2007). *The heart of whiteness: Normal sexuality and race in America, 1880–1940.* Duke University Press.

Central Park Conservancy. (2021a, October 4). *Birding guide.* www.centralparknyc.org/activities/guides/birding

Central Park Conservancy. (2021b, October 4). *The ramble*. www.centralparknyc.org/locations/the-ramble

Chou, R. S., & Taylor, B. (2018). Yellow fever and yellow impotence. In S. Lamb & J. Gilbert (Eds.), *The Cambridge handbook of sexual development* (pp. 241–260). Cambridge University Press. https://doi.org/10.1017/9781108116121.013

Clements, C., & Madrone, S. (2020). Addressing white fragility through mindfulness-based inquiry in sexuality leadership. In J. C. Wadley (Ed.), *Handbook of sexuality leadership: Inspiring community engagement, social empowerment, and transformational influence* (pp. 291–310). Routledge.

Coates, T. (2015). *Between the world and me*. Spiegel & Grau.

Coates, T. (2018, May 7). Kanye west in the age of Donald Trump. *Atlantic*. https://www.theatlantic.com/entertainment/archive/2018/05/im-not-black-im-kanye/559763/

Combahee River Collective. (1977). *The Combahee River Collective statement*. https://americanstudies.yale.edu/sites/default/files/files/Keyword%20Coalition_Readings.pdf

Common Era. (2012). Undoing sex: Against sexual optimism. *LIES: A Journal of Materialist Feminism, 1*(1), 15–34.

Cooper, B. (2016). The racial politics of time [Video]. *TEDWomen*. www.ted.com/talks/brittney_cooper_the_racial_politics_of_time/transcript#t-226805

Cooper, B. (2018). *Eloquent rage: A Black feminist discovers her superpower*. St. Martin's Press.

Crawford, R. (1980). Healthism and the medicalization of everyday life. *International Journal of Health Services, 10*(3), 365–388. https://doi.org/10.2190/3H2H-3XJN-3KAY-G9NY

Creadick, A. (2010). *Perfectly average: The pursuit of normality in postwar America*. University of Massachusetts Press.

Crenshaw, K. (1989). Demarginalizing the intersection of race and sex: A black feminist critique of antidiscrimination doctrine, feminist theory and antiracist politics. *University of Chicago Legal Forum, 1*(8), 139–167.

Curry, T. J. (2017). *The man-not: Race, class, genre, and the dilemmas of black manhood*. Temple University Press.

Davis, F. J. (2001). *Who is black? One nation's definition* (10th anniversary ed.). The Pennsylvania State University Press.

Day-Vines, N. L., Cluxton-Keller, F., Agorsor, C., & Gubara, S. (2021). Strategies for broaching the subjects of race, ethnicity, and culture. *Journal of Counseling & Development, 99*, 348–357. https://onlinelibrary.wiley.com/doi/epdf/10.1002/jcad.12380

Day-Vines, N. L., Cluxton-Keller, F., Agorsor, C., Gubara, S., & Otabil, N. (2020). The multidimensional model of broaching behavior. *Journal of Counseling & Development, 98*(1), 107–118. https://doi.org/10/1002/jcad.12304

Day-Vines, N. L., Wood, S. M., Grothaus, T., Craigen, L., Holman, A., Dotson-Blake, K., & Douglass, M. J. (2007). Broaching the subjects of race, ethnicity, and culture during the counseling process. *Journal of Counseling & Development, 85*(4), 401–409. https://doi.org/10.1002/j.1556-6678.2007.tb00608.x

de Beauvoir, S. (2011). *The second sex* (C. Borde & S. Malovany-Chevallier, Trans.). Vintage Books. (Original work published 1949)

DeGruy, J. (2017). *Post traumatic slave syndrome: America's legacy of enduring injury and healing* (Rev. ed.). Joy DeGruy Publications, Inc.

Delany, S. R. (1999). *Times Square red, Times Square blue*. New York University Press.

Derrida, J. (1976). *Of grammatology* (G. Chakravorty Spivak, Trans.). Johns Hopkins University Press.

Derrida, J. (1978). Structure, sign, and play. In *Writing and difference* (A. Bass, Trans.). The University of Chicago Press.

Diamond, L. (2008). *Sexual fluidity: Understanding women's love and desire*. Harvard University Press.

DiAngelo, R. (2011). White fragility. *International Journal of Critical Pedagogy, 3*(3), 54–70.

DiAngelo, R. (2018). *White fragility: Why it's so hard for white people to talk about racism*. Beacon Press.

Dilley, B. (2015). *This very moment: Teaching, thinking, dancing*. Naropa University Press.

DiValerio, D. M. (2011). *Subversive sainthood and tantric fundamentalism: An historical study of Tibet's holy madmen* [Doctoral dissertation], University of Virginia.

Donegan, M. (2019, February/March). Sex during wartime: The return of Andrea Dworkin's radical vision. *Bookforum, 25,* 5. https://www.bookforum.com/print/2505/the-return-of-andrea-dworkin-s-radical-vision-20623

Dottolo, A. L., & Kaschak, E. (2015). Whiteness and white privilege. *Women & Therapy, 38*(3–4), 179–184.

Dreyfus, H. L. (1991). *Being-in-the-world: A commentary on Heidegger's being and time, Division I*. The MIT Press.

Duggan, L. (2002). The new homonormativity: The sexual politics of neoliberalism. In R. Castronovo & D. D. Nelson (Eds.), *Materializing democracy: Toward a revitalized cultural politics* (pp. 175–194). Duke University Press.

Dunn, C. D. Somborac, T., & Akpunar, B. A. (2020). We're in this together: Sensation of the host cell environment by endosymbiotic bacteria. In M. Kloc (Ed.), *Symbiosis: Cellular, molecular, medical and evolutionary aspects – Results and problems in cell differentiation* (Vol. 69, pp. 179–198). Springer.

Dutton, D. G., & Painter, S. (1993). Emotional attachments in abusive relationships: A test of traumatic bonding theory. *Violence and Victims, 8*(2), 105–120.

Dweck, C. S. (2006). *Mindset: The new psychology of success*. Random House.

Dworkin, A. (1974). *Woman hating: A radical look at sexuality*. E.P. Dutton.

Dworkin, A. (1989). *Pornography: Men possessing women*. Plume. (Original work published 1979)

Dworkin, A. (2006). *Intercourse*. Basic Books. (Original work published 1987)

Ehlers, N. (2012). *Racial imperatives: Discipline, performativity, and struggles against subjection*. Indiana University Press.

Ehrenreich, B. (2009). *Bright-sided: How positive thinking is undermining America*. Picador.

Eig, J. (2014). *The birth of the pill: How four crusaders reinvented sex and launched a revolution*. W. W. Norton and Company.

Ellison, M. M. (1996). *Erotic justice: A liberating ethic of sexuality*. Westminster John Knox Press.

Embodiment Matters. (2020, December 4). *Serious mind vs. play mind*. https://embodimentmatters.com/?s=Norbu

Eng, D. L. (2010). *The feeling of kinship: Queer liberalism and the racialization of intimacy*. Duke University Press.

Eng, D. L., & Han, S. (2019). *Racial melancholia, racial dissociation.* Duke University Press.

Epstein, S. (1999). Gay and lesbian movements in the United States: Dilemmas of identity, diversity and political strategy. In B. Adam, et al. (Eds.), *The global emergence of gay and lesbian politics* (pp. 30–90). Temple University Press.

Fanon, F. (1986). *Black skin, white masks.* Pluto Press. (Original work published 1967)

Felski, R. (2000). *Doing time: Feminist theory and postmodern culture.* New York University Press.

Fern, J. (2020). *Polysecure: Attachment, trauma and consensual nonmonogamy.* Thorntree Press.

Fodero, L. W. (2012, September 13). In Central Park, a birders' secluded haven comes with a dark side. *The New York Times.* www.nytimes.com/2012/09/14/nyregion/in-central-park-an-uneasy-coexistence-grows-uneasier.html

Foucault, M. (1990). *The history of sexuality: Volume 1: An introduction* (R. Hurley, Trans.). Vintage. (Original work published 1976)

Foucault, M. (1994). *The birth of the clinic: An archaeology of medical perception* (A. M. Sheridan Smith, Trans.). Vintage Books. (Original work published 1963)

Foucault, M. (1997). *Ethics: Subjectivity and truth. Essential works of Michel Foucault* (Vol. 1) (P. Hurley, Trans.). (P. Rabinow, Ed.). New Press.

Frankenberg, R. (1997). Introduction: Local whitenesses, localizing whiteness. In R. Frankenberg (Ed.), *Displacing whiteness: Essays in social and cultural criticism* (pp. 1–34). Duke University Press. https://doi.org/10.2307/j.ctv1220r19.3

Freeman, E. (2010). *Time binds: Queer temporalities, queer histories.* Duke University Press.

Freud, S. (1920). *Three essays on the theory of sexuality* (2nd ed., A. A. Brill, Trans.). Nervous and Mental Disease Publishing Co. (Original work published 1905) www.globalgrey.co.uk

Gabosch, A., & Shub, J. (Eds.). (2019). *Sex-positive now.* Sexy Activist Publishing.

Gabriel, J. (2000). Dreaming of a white. . . . In S. Cottle (Ed.), *Ethnic minorities and the media* (pp. 67–83). Open University Press.

Gagnon, J. H. (2004). *An interpretation of desire: Essays in the study of sexuality.* University of Chicago Press. (Original work published 1974)

Gagnon, J. H., & Simon, W. (1973). *Sexual conduct: The social sources of human sexuality.* Aldine.

Garriott, P. O., Reiter, S., & Brownfield, J. (2015). Testing the efficacy of brief multicultural education interventions in white college students. *Journal of Diversity in Higher Education, 9*(2), 158–169. https://doi.org/10.1037/a0039547

Garvey Berger, J. (2012). *Changing on the job: Developing leaders for a complex world.* Stanford University Press.

Gentles-Peart, K. (2018). Controlling beauty ideals: Caribbean women, thick bodies, and White supremacist discourse. *WSQ: Women's Studies Quarterly, 46*(1–2), 199–214.

Gilman, S. L. (1985). Black bodies, white bodies: Toward an iconography of female sexuality in the late nineteenth-century art, medicine, and literature. *Critical Inquiry, 12*(1), 204–242.

Glave, T. (2000). A real place. In *Whose song? And other stories* (pp. 183–193). City Lights.

Glick, E. (2000). Sex-positive: Feminism, queer theory, and the politics of transgression. *Feminist Review, 64*(1), 19–45. https://doi.org/10.1080/014177800338936

Glickman, C. (2019). The principles of sex-positivity. In A. Gabosch & J. Shub (Eds.), *Sex-positive now* (pp. 20–23). Sexy Activist Publishing.

Greenberg, G. (2014). *The book of woe: The DSM and the unmaking of psychiatry.* Blue Rider Press.

Greyston Bakery. (2021, March 29). *Open hiring: Why it's worked at Greyston bakery.* https://greyston.org/open-hiring-why-its-worked-at-greyston-bakery/

Grzanka, P. R., Frantell, K. A., & Fassinger, R. E. (2020). The white racial affect scale (WRAS): A measure of white guilt, shame, and negation. *The Counseling Psychologist, 48*(1), 47–77. https://doi.org/10.1177/0011000019878808

Guy-Shefthall, B. (1995). The body politic: Sexuality, violence, reproduction – Introduction. In B. Guy-Shefthall (Ed.), *Words of fire: An anthology of African-American feminist thought* (p. 359). The New York Press.

Halberstam, J. (2005). *In a queer time and place: Transgender bodies, subcultural lives.* New York University Press.

Halberstam, J. (2011). *The queer art of failure.* Duke University Press.

Halberstam, J. (2020). *Wild things: The disorder of desire.* Duke University Press.

Halberstam, J. (2021, May 23). *On destitution, dereliction, depreciation and dispossession: Unbuild the world!* [Keynote address]. 27th Annual Lavender Languages and Linguistics Conference. California Institute of Integral Studies, San Francisco, CA. https://www.youtube.com/watch?v=uSn9om6tbI4

Hale, E. G. (1998). *Making whiteness: The culture of segregation in the south, 1890–1940.* Vintage Books.

Hanh, T. N. (2017a). *The art of living: Peace and freedom in the here and now.* Harper One.

Hanh, T. N. (2017b, August 2). The insight of interbeing: Everything relies on everything else in order to manifest. *Timeless Wisdom.* www.garrisoninstitute.org/blog/insight-of-interbeing/

Hardy, J. W., & Easton, D. (2019). *The ethical slut* (3rd ed.). Ten Speed Press.

Hare-Mustin, R. T. (1994). Discourses in the mirrored room: A postmodern analysis of therapy. *Family Process, 33*, 19–35.

Harris, C. (1993). Whiteness as property. *Harvard Law Review, 106*(8), 1707–1791.

Hartog, F. (2015). *Regimes of historicity: Presentism and experiences of time* (S. Brown, Trans.). Columbia University Press. https://doi.org/10.7312/hart16376

Hegel, W. F. (1956). *The philosophy of history* (J. Sibree, Trans.). Dover Books. (Original work published 1899)

Heidegger, M. (2008). *Being and time* (J. Macquarrie & E. Robinson, Trans.). Harper and Row Publishers. (Original work published 1962)

Henriques, M. (2019, March 26). Can the legacy of trauma be passed down the generations? *BBC News.* www.bbc.com/future/article/20190326-what-is-epigenetics

Herz, M., & Johansson, T. (2015). The normativity of the concept of heteronormativity. *Journal of Homosexuality, 62,* 1009–1020.

Higginbotham, E. B. (1993). *Righteous discontent: The women's movement in the Black Baptist Church, 1880–1920.* Harvard University Press.

Hite, S. (2004). *The Hite report: A nationwide study of female sexuality.* Seven Stories Press. (Original work published 1976)

Ho, K. (2009). *Liquidated: An ethnography of Wall Street.* Duke University Press.

Hook, D. (2001). Therapeutic discourse, co-construction, interpellation, role-induction: Psychotherapy as iatrogenic treatment modality? *International Journal of Psychotherapy,*

6(1), 47–66. https://doi.org/10.1080/13569080120042207; www.tandfonline.com/doi/abs/10.1080/13569080120042207

Iantaffi, A. (2012). White privilege in sex and relationship therapy [Editorial]. *Sexual and Relational Therapy*, *27*(2), 99–102.

Iasenza, S. (2010). What's queer about sex. *Family Process*, *49*(3), 291–308.

Irvine, J. (2005). *Disorders of desire: Sex and gender in modern American sexology*. Temple University Press. (Original work published 1990)

Ivanski, C., & Kohut, T. (2017). Exploring definitions of sex-positivity through thematic analysis. *The Canadian Journal of Human Sexuality*, *26*(3), 216–225. https://doi.org/10.3138/cjhs.2

Jackson, S., & Scott, S. (2010). *Theorizing sexuality*. McGraw Hill and Open University Press.

Jaipur Literature Festival. (2020, September 2). Natalie Avalos, Jeanine Canty, & Enrique Sepulveda: Dismantling racism through decolonizing systems [Video]. *YouTube*. https://www.youtube.com/watch?v=J6F8oswLxro

Jagose, A. (1996). *Queer theory: An introduction*. New York University Press.

Jawaid, A., Roszkowski, M., & Mansuy, I. M. (2018). Transgenerational epigenetics of traumatic stress. *Progress in Molecular Biology Translational Science*, *158*, 273–298.

Jones-Rogers, S. E. (2019). *They were her property: White women as slave owners in the American south*. Yale University Press.

Kapil, B. (2001). *The vertical interrogation of strangers*. Kelsey Street Press.

Kashdan, T., & Biswas-Diener, R. (2014). *The upside of your dark side: Why being your whole self—not just your "good" self—drives success and fulfillment*. Plume.

Katz, J. N. (1995). *The invention of heterosexuality*. Dulton Books.

Kendi, I. X. (2016). *Stamped from the beginning: The definitive history of racist ideas in America*. Bold Type Books.

Kendi, I. X. (2019). *How to be an antiracist*. One World.

King, J. E. (1991). Dysconscious racism: Ideology, identity, and the miseducation of teachers. *The Journal of Negro Education*, *60*(2), 133–146.

Kleinplatz, P. J., Charest, M., Paradis, N., Ellis, M., Rosen, L., Ménard, D., & Ramsay, T. O. (2020). Treatment of low sexual desire or frequency using a sexual enhancement group couples therapy approach. *Journal of Sexual Medicine*, *17*, 1288–1296.

Kleinplatz, P. J., & Ménard, A. D. (2007). Building blocks towards optimal sexuality: Constructing a conceptual model. *The Family Journal: Counseling and Therapy for Couples and Families*, *15*, 72–78.

Kleinplatz, P. J., & Ménard, A. D. (2020). *Magnificent sex: Lessons from extraordinary lovers*. Routledge.

Kleinplatz, P. J., Ménard, A. D., Paquet, M. P., Paradis, N. Campbell, M. Zuccarino, D., & Mehak, L. (2009). The components of optimal sexuality: A portrait of "great sex." *The Canadian Journal of Human Sexuality*, *18*, 1–13.

Kloc, M. (2020). *Symbiosis: Cellular, molecular, medical and evolutionary aspects – Results and problems in cell differentiation* (Vol. 69). Springer.

Kottler, J. A. (2005). *Divine madness: Ten stories of creative struggle*. John Wiley & Sons.

Lacal, I., & Ventura, R. (2018, September 28). Epigenetic inheritance: Concepts, mechanisms and perspectives. *Frontiers in Molecular Neuroscience*. https://doi.org/10.3389/fnmol.2018.00292

Laqueur, T. (1990). *Making sex: Body and gender from the Greeks to Freud.* Harvard University Press.

Levenson, E. (2021, March 30). Former officer knelt on George Floyd for 9 minutes and 29 seconds – Not the infamous 8:46. *CNN.* www.cnn.com/2021/03/29/us/george-floyd-timing-929-846/index.html

Levine, P. (1997). Waking the tiger: The innate experience to transform overwhelming experiences. North Atlantic Books.

Libby, R. (2016, June 30). We need a sex-positive revolution [Video file]. *TEDx Western Washington University.* https://www.youtube.com/watch?v=gpcA1wn0cEQ

Lipsitz, G. (2018). *The possessive investment in whiteness: How white people profit from identity politics* (20th anniversary ed.). Temple University Press. (Original work published 1998)

Livingston, J. (Director) (1991). *Paris is burning* [Film]. Academy Entertainment, Off White Productions.

Loliya, K. (2019). The negative in sex positive. In A. Gabosch and J. Shub (Eds.), *Sex positive now: An anthology of movers and shakers in the world of sexuality* (pp. 31–36). Sexy Activist Publishing.

Lomax, T. (2018). *Jezebel unhinged: Loosing the black female body in religion and culture.* Duke University Press.

Lorde, A. (2007). Uses of the erotic. In *Sister outsider.* Ten Speed Press. (Original work Published in 1984)

Lowe, L. (2015). *The intimacies of four continents.* Duke University Press.

Madrone, S., & Clements, C. (2021). White fragility and decolonizing sexuality research. In G. Herdt, M. Marzullo & N. Polen Petit (Eds.), *Critical sexual literacy: Forecasting trends in sexual politics, diversity and pedagogy* (pp. 73–77). Anthem Press.

Marzullo, M. (2011). Through a glass, darkly: U.S. marriage discourse and neoliberalism. *Journal of Homosexuality, 58*(6–7), 758–774.

Maslin Nir, S. (2020, June 14). How 2 lives collided in Central Park, rattling the nation. *The New York Times.* www.nytimes.com/2020/06/14/nyregion/central-park-amy-cooper-christian-racism.html

Maslow, A. (1943). A theory of human motivation. *Psychological Review, 50*(2), 370–396. https://doi.org/10.1037/h0054346

Menakem, R. (2017). *My grandmother's hands: Racialized trauma and the pathway to mending our hearts and bodies.* Central Recovery Press.

Menakem, R. (2020, June 4). Notice the rage; notice the silence. *On Being With Kristin Tippett. On Being.* https://onbeing.org/programs/resmaa-menakem-notice-the-rage-notice-the-silence/

Merleau-Ponty, M. (2012). *Phenomenology of perception.* Routledge. (Original work published 1945)

Millbank, L. (2012). *The ethical prude: Imagining an authentic sex-negative feminism. A radical transfeminist.* https://radtransfem.wordpress.com/2012/02/29/the-ethical-prude-imagining-an-authentic-sex-negative-feminism/#whyreclaim

Miller, R. (2022). *Intimate relationships* (9th ed.). McGraw Hill.

Mohanram, R. (1999). *Black-body: Women, colonialism, and space.* University of Minnesota Press.

Morgan, J. L. (1997). "Some could suckle over their shoulder": Male travelers, female bodies, and the gendering of racial ideology, 1500–1770. *William and Mary Quarterly, 54*(1), 167–192.

Morrison, T. (1987). *Beloved*. Alfred A. Knopf.

Mosher, C. (2017). Historical perspectives of sex-positivity: Contributing to a new paradigm within counseling psychology. *The Counseling Psychologist, 45*(4), 487–503.

Muller, J. (2020, June 5). My tiny, white town just held a protest [Editorial]. We're not alone. *Washington Post*. www.washingtonpost.com/opinions/2020/06/05/my-tiny-white-town-just-held-protest-were-not-alone/

Muñoz, J. E. (1999). *Disidentifications: Queers of color and the performance of politics*. University of Minnesota Press.

Muñoz, J. E. (2009). *Cruising utopia: The then and there of queer futurity*. New York University Press.

Musser, G. (2018, May 9). What is spacetime? *Nature*. www.nature.com/articles/d41586-018-05095-z

Nagoski, E. (2015). *Come as you are: The surprising new science that will transform your sex life*. Simon and Schuster.

Nagoski, E. (2018). The truth about unwanted arousal [Video]. *TEDTalk*. www.ted.com/talks/emily_nagoski_the_truth_about_unwanted_arousal?language=en#t-204720

Neff, K. (2020). *Sex-positive: Redefining our attitudes to love and sex*. Watkins.

Nelson, M. (2021). *On freedom: Four songs of care and constraint*. Graywolf Press.

Newman, L. M. (1999). *White women's rights: The racial origins of feminism in the United States*. Oxford University Press.

Ng, S., Wright, R., & Kuper, A. (2019). The divergence and convergence of critical reflection and critical reflexivity: Implications for health professions education. *Academic Medicine, 94*(8), 1122–1128.

Norbu, T. (1998). *Magic dance: The display of the self-nature of the five wisdom Dakinis*. Shambhala.

Osler, J. (n.d.). *Opportunities for white people in the fight for racial justice: Moving from actor >ally > accomplice*. www.whiteaccomplices.org/

Owen, E. (2019). *The art of flaneuring: How to wander with intention and discover a better life*. Tiller Press.

Owens, R. (2020). *Love and rage: The path of liberation through anger*. North Atlantic Books.

Painter, N. I. (2010). *The history of white people*. W. W. Norton & Company.

Perel, E. (2006). *Mating in captivity: Reconciling the erotic and the domestic*. HarperCollins.

Phillips, D. T. (2020). Belonging. In P. A. Yetunde & C. A. Giles (Eds.), *Black and Buddhist: What Buddhism can teach us about race, resilience, transformation and freedom* (pp. 82–96). Shambhala.

Queen, C. (2002). *Real live nude girl: Chronicles of sex-positive culture* (2nd ed.). Cleis Press. (Original work published 1997)

Rabelo, V. C., Robotham, K. J., & McCluney, C. L. (2021). "Against a sharp white background": How black women experience the white gaze at work. *Gender, Work, Organizations, 28*, 1840–1858.

Racially and Ethnically Motivated Violent Extremism: The Transnational Threat. (2021). *United States house of representatives: Subcommittee on intelligence and counterterrorism of the committee on homeland security*. www.govinfo.gov/content/pkg/CHRG-117hhrg44824/html/CHRG-117hhrg44824.htm

Ramoya, M. C. B. (2016.). Difference, dissemination, destinerrance, and geocatastrophe. *Philosophia, 17*(1), 69–92.

Rankine, C. (2019). On blondness and whiteness. In D. C. Blight (Ed.), *The image of whiteness* (pp. 172–179). SPBH Editions and Art on the Underground.

Rich, A. (1980). Compulsory heterosexuality and lesbian existence. *Signs: Journal of Women in Culture and Society, 5*(4), 631–660.

Rottenberg, C. (2003). "Passing:" Race, identification, and desire. *Criticism, 45*(4), 435–452. www.jstor.org/stable/23126398

Russell-Brown, K. (2009). *The color of crime.* New York University Press.

Saini, A. (2019). *The return of race science.* Beacon Press.

Scharmer, O. (2019, April 15). Vertical literacy: Reimagining the 21st-century university. Field of the future. *Presencing Institute.* https://medium.com/presencing-institute-blog/vertical-literacy-12-principles-for-reinventing-the-21st-century-university-39c2948192ee

Schnarch, D. (2009). *Intimacy and desire: Awaken the passion in your relationship.* Beaufort Books.

Schuller, K. (2021). *The trouble with white women: A counterhistory of feminism.* Public Affairs.

Selassie, S. (2020). Turning toward myself. In P. A. Yetunde & C. A. Giles (Eds.), *Black and Buddhist: What Buddhism can teach us about race, resilience, transformation and freedom* (pp. 97–118). Shambhala.

Sen, R. (2007, July 10). Are immigrants and refugees people of color? *ColorLines.* https://colorlines.com/article/are-immigrants-and-refugees-people-color/

Senge, P. M., Scharmer, C. O., Jaworski, J., & Flowers, B. S. (2004). *Presence: Human purpose and the field of the future.* Doubleday.

Serra, D. (2019). Looking ahead: Justice and the future of sex positivity. In A. Gabosch and J. Shub (Eds.), *Sex positive now: An anthology of movers and shakers in the world of sexuality* (pp. 213–215). Sexy Activist Publishing.

Simon, W., & Gagnon, J. H. (1969). On psychosexual development. In D. A. Goslin (Ed.), *Handbook of socialization theory and research* (pp. 60–67). Rand McNally.

Simon, W., & Gagnon, J. H. (1986). Sexual scripts: Permanence and change. *Archives of Sexual Behavior, 13,* 97–120.

Simon, W., & Gagnon, J. H. (2003). Sexual scripts: Origins, influences and changes. *Qualitative Sociology, 26,* 491–497. https://doi.org/10.1023/B:QUAS.0000005053.99846.e5

Simply Sexy Editorial Team (2014, September 2). *Interview with Dr. Roger Libby on Sex Positivity.* https://simplysxy.com/articles/2014/09/02/interview-with-dr-roger-libby-creator-of-the-term-sex-positivity/

Skibba, R. (2019, May 20). The disturbing resilience of scientific racism. *Smithsonian Magazine.* https://www.smithsonianmag.com/science-nature/disturbing-resilience-scientific-racism-180972243/

Spanierman, L. B., Beard, J. C., & Todd, N. R. (2012). White men's fears, White women's tears: Examining gender differences in racial affect types. *Sex Roles, 67,* 174–186. https://doi.org/10.1007/s11199-012-0162-2

Spanierman, L. B., & Cabrera, N. L. (2015). The emotions of White racism and anti-racism. In V. Watson, D. Howard-Wagner & L. Spanierman (Eds.), *Unveiling whiteness in the twenty-first century: Global manifestations, transdisciplinary interventions* (pp. 9–28). Lexington Books.

Spanierman, L. B., & Heppner, M. J. (2004). Psychosocial costs of racism to whites scale (PCRW): Construction and initial validation. *Journal of Counseling Psychology, 51,* 249–262. https://doi.org/10.1037/0022-0167.51.2.249

Spanierman, L. B., Todd, N. R., & Anderson, C. J. (2009). Psychosocial costs of racism to Whites: Understanding patterns among university students. *Journal of Counseling Psychology, 56*, 239–252. https://doi.org/10.1037/a0015432

Stamper, N. (2005). *Breaking rank: A top cop's exposé of the dark side of American policing.* Avalon Press.

Starkey, B. S. (2015). *In defense of Uncle Tom: Why Blacks must police racial loyalty.* Cambridge University Press.

Starkey, B. S. (2016, December 12). *Respectability politics: How a flawed conversation sabotages black lives.* https://theundefeated.com/features/respectability-politics-how-a-flawed-conversation-sabotages-black-lives/

Stember, C. H. (1978). *Sexual racism: The emotional barrier to an integrated society.* Harper Colophon.

Stephens, E. (2015). The object of normality: The "search for Norma" competition (Conference Paper). *ResearchGate.* file:///C:/Users/Owner/Downloads/The_Object_of_Normality_The_Search_for_N.pdf

Stephens, E. (2018). The normal body on display: Public exhibitions of the Norma and Normman statues. In C. Smith, F. Attwood & B. McNair (Eds.), *The Routledge companion to media, sex and sexuality* (pp. 7–18). Routledge. https://doi.org/10.4324/9781315168302-2

Stern, R. (2021, February 24). Interview with Resmaa Menakem, author of My Grandmother's Hands. *gal-dem.* https://gal-dem.com/trauma-decontextualised-in-a-people-can-look-like-culture-resmaa-menakem-on-how-racism-affects-the-body/

Stokes, M. (2001). *The color of sex: Whiteness, heterosexuality and the fictions of white supremacy.* Duke University Press.

Strings, S. (2019). *Fearing the black-body: The racial origins of fat phobia.* New York University Press.

Sue, D. W., Lin, A. I., Torino, G. C., Capodilupo, C. M., & Rivera, D. P. (2009). Racial microaggressions and difficult dialogues on race in the classroom. *Cultural Diversity and Ethnic Minority Psychology, 15*(2), 183. https://doi.org/10.1037/a0014191

Tatkin, S. (2012). *Wired for love: How understanding your partner's brain and attachment style can help you defuse conflict and build a secure relationship.* New Harbinger Publications.

Taylor, Y. (2011). Complexities and complications: Intersections of class and sexuality. In Y. Taylor, S. Hines & M. Casey (Eds.), *Theorizing intersectionality and sexuality* (pp. 37–53). Palgrave Macmillan.

Taylor, Y., Hines, S., & Casey, M. (Eds). (2011). *Theorizing intersectionality and sexuality* (pp. 37–53). Palgrave Macmillan.

Thorne, K. S. (2013, February 5). What is space and time continuum [Video]. *YouTube.* www.youtube.com/watch?v=mvdlN4H4T54

Tilsen, J. (2021). *Queering your therapy practice: Queer theory, narrative therapy, and imagining new identities.* Routledge.

Todd, N. R., Spanierman, L. B., & Poteat, V. P. (2011). Longitudinal examination of the psychosocial costs of racism to Whites across the college experience. *Journal of Counseling Psychology, 58*, 508–521. https://doi.org/10.1037/a0025066

Trungpa, C. (2008). *True perception: The path of dharma art* (J. L. Lief, Ed.). Shambhala. (Original work published 1996)

Veaux, F., & Rickert, E. (2014). *More than two: A practical guide to ethical polyamory.* Thorntree Press.

Wade, J. (2004). *Transcendent sex: When lovemaking opens the veil*. Paraview.

Watter, D. N. (2012). Ethics and sex therapy: A neglected dimension. In P. Kleinplatz (Ed.), *New directions in sex therapy* (pp. 85–99). Routledge.

Wilkerson, I. (2020). *Caste: The origins of our discontents*. Random House.

Williams, D. J., Prior, E., & Wegner, J. (2013). Resolving social problems associated with Sexuality. Can a "sex-positive" approach help? *Social Work, 58*(3), 273–276.

Wilson, M. (2022, May 16). They were at Tops when the shooting started. This is how they survived. *The New York Times*. www.nytimes.com/2022/05/16/nyregion/buffalo-shooting-tops-employees.html

Wong, W. (2021, August 4). White woman in viral video says she had no choice but to call police on Black bird-watcher. *NBC News*. https://www.nbcnews.com/news/us-news/white-woman-viral-video-says-she-had-no-choice-call-n1275898

Yetunde, P. A. (2020). Voluntary segregation: The paradox, promise, and peril of people of color sanghas. In P. A. Yetunde & C. A. Giles (Eds.), *Black and Buddhist: What Buddhism can teach us about race, resilience, transformation and freedom* (pp. 97–118). Shambhala.

Index

For Product Safety Concerns and Information please contact our EU
representative GPSR@taylorandfrancis.com
Taylor & Francis Verlag GmbH, Kaufingerstraße 24, 80331 München, Germany